R.M.Kliment & Frances Halsband Architects

THE MASTER ARCHITECT SERIES

R.M.Kliment & Frances Halsband Architects

images
Publishing

Published in Australia in 2008 by
The Images Publishing Group Pty Ltd
ABN 89 059 734 431
6 Bastow Place, Mulgrave, Victoria 3170, Australia
Tel: +61 3 9561 5544 Fax: +61 3 9561 4860
books@imagespublishing.com
www.imagespublishing.com

Copyright © The Images Publishing Group Pty Ltd 2008
The Images Publishing Group Reference Number: 713

National Library of Australia Cataloguing-in-Publication entry:

R.M. Kliment & Frances Halsband Architects, revisited.

ISBN 978 1 86470 1302 (hbk.).

1. R.M. Kliment & Frances Halsband Architects.
2. Architecture, American. 3. Architecture – United States –
21st century. I. R.M. Kliment & Frances Halsband
Architects. (Series: Master architect series).

720.973

Edited by Melina Deliyannis

Designed by The Graphic Image Studio Pty Ltd, Mulgrave, Australia
www.tgis.com.au

Digital production by Splitting Image Colour Studio Pty Ltd, Australia

Printed by Everbest Printing Co. Ltd., Hong Kong/China

IMAGES has included on its website a page for special notices in relation to this and its other
publications. Please visit www.imagespublishing.com

Contents

Introduction

Reflections, Responses, Transformations:
The Architecture of R.M.Kliment & Frances Halsband Architects

Long Island Rail Road Entrance Pavilion

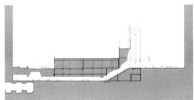

Long Island Rail Road Entrance Pavilion section

The German philosopher and passionate *flaneur*, Walter Benjamin, once reminded his readers that besides the "attentive concentration of a tourist before a famous building" there needed to be another form of appreciation for architecture: one of "tactile appropriation," of "touch," rather than sight, of "use" and "habit." This encounter with architecture usually happened, he wrote, "much less through rapt attention than by noticing the object in incidental fashion,"[1] even in a heightened state of distraction.

At a time when deliberately spectacular and entertaining architecture seems to be all that the public notices and talks about, it is worth recalling Benjamin's admonition. The office of R.M.Kliment & Frances Halsband Architects in New York, has, since its founding in 1972, produced work that has consistently managed to cater to both forms of architectural appreciation: it has inserted itself in its urban environment with great confidence, and the rapt attention of an interested observer reliably reveals layer after layer of carefully considered references and details that speak to the intense engagement of its architects with context and historic precedent.

At the same time, however, the office is perfectly happy to produce buildings that work so seamlessly, are so easily used and inhabited, and convincingly pleasant to all of our senses, that their users might, after a short while, not notice them anymore, just like perfectly fitting clothes.

To most of the countless commuters, who cross the Long Island Rail Road entrance pavilion at 34th Street and 7th Avenue at rush hour in New York City, the elegant building has probably become almost invisible. Its glass tower might briefly serve as a beacon of orientation, but most passengers move through it in a heightened state of distraction on their way to and from the maze of underground passages that make up today's Pennsylvania Station—and that are so utterly devoid of charm and design intent. To the occasional *flaneur*, however, who lingers for a moment between sidewalk and escalators, the building offers rich rewards. Its tall, luminous glass shaft extends vertically, roughly equal in height to the depth below. Behind a sidewalk-deep, elegantly suspended canopy, it emerges from a patterned brick coat that carries technical equipment in the back. During the day, the space is filled

1 Walter Benjamin, "The Work of Art in the Age of Mechanical Reproduction," 1936.

with the light of the New York sky; at night, floodlighting turns it into a softly glowing magic lantern. A heavy, four-sided clock hangs freely on long cables all the way from the 50-foot ceiling, swinging slightly in the air current above the hurried passengers: a striking instance of urban iconography whose almost cinematographic presence suggests the precarious nature of time and, naturally, evokes memories of the old Penn Station, from whose enormous glass vaults it came. Only here, some of the magic that the old station represented, can still be found. Kliment & Halsband were keenly aware of the great tradition of entrances to underground railways, from Norman Foster's evocatively slanted tubes emerging out of Bilbao's sidewalks, to Charles Holden's splendid modernist work in 1930's London, and all the way back to Hector Guimard's famous Parisian examples at the turn of the century. Just like them, they remind us of the days when traveling by train was still a profoundly moving experience, accomplishing the "miracle ... whereby scenes which hitherto have had no existence save in our minds are about to become the scenes among which we shall be living ..." as Marcel Proust so aptly put it.[2]

This building perfectly represents Kliment & Halsband's architectural ethos. While functioning so effortlessly that it is instantly appropriated by its users—and often noticed only in a state of distraction—a second look and attentive concentration on it unfailingly reveal a deep engagement with the site and its history, and with the poetic and metaphorical urban iconography that has resulted from architectural, literary, and cinematic efforts over the last 100 years. The firm's architecture is one of calmness, subtlety, integrity, and depth; of profound historical knowledge and a culture of understatement and humility. Instead of insisting on a "K&H style" that would be applied to any given project, they meet every project on its own terms. After all, as Alfred Hitchcock once remarked, "style is merely self plagiarism."

The recent Henry A. Wallace Visitor and Education Center at the Franklin D. Roosevelt Presidential Library in Hyde Park, New York, is another case in point. President Roosevelt had taken great interest in the design of the library and worked closely with the architects Henry A. Toombs and Louis Simon, in the 1930s, to create a group of modest

Franklin D. Roosevelt Presidential Library

2 Marcel Proust on the Gare St. Lazare, in: *Remembrance of Things Past* (New York: Vintage, 1919, 1982), p. 694.

Arcadia University's Landman Library

U.S. Post Office and Courthouse

Yale Divinity School

Dutch Colonial buildings with rough field-stone walls. He explained that this was an architecture that symbolized endurance against great odds, quiet determination, and artistry for all time to come. He felt that the humility and decency of this architecture represented best his own style and ambition; an understanding of the role of the president that unfailingly evokes nostalgia 70 years later. Kliment & Halsband continued this tradition. Its visitor center of four seemingly separate buildings with their protruding, translucent roofs on wooden columns, frame an interior court whose calmness and restraint is reminiscent of a rural monastery's central cloister. Again, the project's strength stems from its intelligent and insightful dialogue with the existing architecture; from an understanding of the site and its history. While the new buildings' exteriors respond to the Dutch Colonial style of their predecessors, their interiors apply the walls' suggestion of a readable construction to the open truss work that adorns the light and airy spaces of classrooms and meeting halls throughout. They are calm and self-assured, neither fashionable nor spectacular.

Most of the projects of Kliment & Halsband have been new buildings in dense urban or campus contexts, or extensions to, and restorations of, existing buildings. In each case, the firm provides reliably engaged dialogues with the existing history, with the site, and its narrative. The architects prove to be exceptional conversationalists, both in person and in their architectural ethic: they listen, they respond, they don't overwhelm their counterpart with their own agenda, instead, they contribute and enrich. They provide the most erudite and intelligent response any partner in a dialogue could hope for.

When perusing the firm's work, one is bound to make countless discoveries. At Arcadia University's Landman Library in Glenside, Pennsylvania, we suddenly, amidst delightful bright and open reading rooms, find a nod to Alvar Aalto's Viipuri Library of 1935; the Court Clerk's intake hall of the Brooklyn Post Office and Courthouse renovation seems to reference Otto Wagner's 1903 Postal Savings Bank in Vienna. When Kliment & Halsband began to work at Yale's Divinity School—Delano & Aldrich's delightful 1930's re-rendering

Franklin & Marshall, Roschel Performing Arts Center

Primary School 178

Primary School 54

State University of New York at Albany

of Jefferson's great lawn at University of Virginia—open, tall spaces emerged that the original architects did not foresee, but are now as integral and convincing as if they had always been there.

The Franklin & Marshall College, Roschel Performing Arts Center in Lancaster, Pennsylvania, inserts itself among its neighbors, reusing part of an adjacent former pool and providing new circulation and performance spaces. While listening carefully to what the existing red brick buildings have to say, to their scale and materials, the curved, columnar façade of the new lobby calmly refers to similar motives at, for instance, Dresden's Opera or Vienna's Burgtheater, and so quietly signal to the campus the role of its new building.

New York City Primary School 178, close to the Cloisters, engages in a convincing dialogue with the brick-clad housing blocks that surround it. The changes to their somewhat tired formal language are subtle, but powerful: while using the same height, the proportions and layout of the windows confidently speak a fresh new dialect, as does the changing treatment of street and side façades, the fourth-floor gymnasium, and the second-floor kindergarten playground. Its companion piece, Primary School 54, is organized in relation to the distant landscape, opening the corridors to views of downtown New York and the passing commuter trains, and linking children with the life of a great city beyond their immediate neighborhood.

The successful and enriching conversation between new and old could hardly be more convincing than at the restoration of the Arts and Sciences Building at the State University of New York, Albany. An elegant, 25-foot-tall glazed A-frame leads the visitor to newly designed underground spaces; it does not compete with the existing Edward Durrell Stone architecture surrounding it, but still confidently confirms its presence. The ingenious new lighting scheme engages the concave concrete skin between the columns of Stone's typical arrangement by using them as reflectors at night. For the first time, it seems, the existing 1968 architecture has fully come into its own.

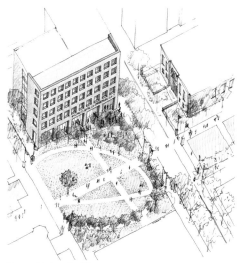
Brown University Plan

As significant as they are invisible—at least at first sight—are those projects where the firm plans the frameworks that will then let buildings by others emerge at the right place, size, structure, and format in a complex context. At Brown University, where Frances Halsband became architect advisor to the board and master planner in 2002, her definition of spaces for the university's future growth changed the way the campus functions. A sequence of quadrangles along a new north–south axis will redirect growth, stitch separate parts of the campus back together, and provide a satisfying urban environment for Providence's East Side neighborhood.

In recent years, the Finnish architect and critic Juhani Pallasmaa and others have returned to Benjamin's point and noticed the "ocular-centrism of our culture" and in particular the "ocular bias" of architecture. Pallasmaa demanded to complement "the city of the eye" with a "haptic city," to allow for architecture as a multi-sensory experience that includes the richness of history's many layers and metaphors. His words could not be more fitting in regard to the philosophy behind Kliment & Halsband's work: "The timeless task of architecture is to create embodied and lived existential metaphors that concretize and structure our being in the world … Buildings and towns enable us to structure, understand and remember the shapeless flow of reality and, ultimately, to recognize and remember who we are." [3]

Dietrich Neumann

Dietrich Neumann has been a professor for the history of architecture at Brown University since 1990. He has trained as an architect in Munich and London and received his PhD in the history of architecture at the University of Munich. He publishes frequently on 19th- and 20th-century European and American architecture.

3 Juhani Pallasmaa, _The Eyes of the Skin_ (Chichester: John Wiley & Sons Ltd. 2005), pp. 19ff and 71.

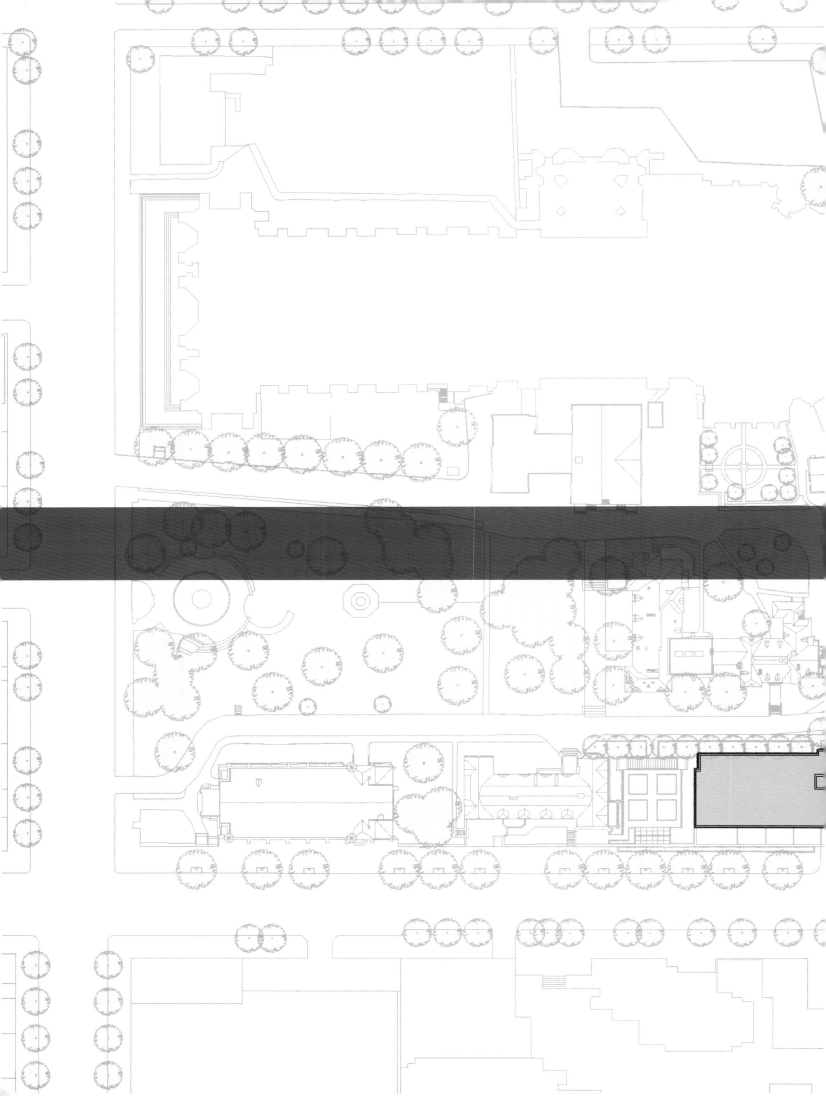

Selected Works 1996–2007

1

1   View from southeast
2   Site plan

Bronx, New York

New York City Board of Education

82,000 square feet

Design 1995/Completion 1999

Steel frame, concrete-filled metal deck

Brick, cast stone portals, coping, and capstones, painted steel fences, gates, and rails, painted aluminum windows, standing seam metal roof, painted wallboard, structural glazed facing tile, wood doors, acoustical tile ceiling

Primary School 54

This new school accommodates 622 students in pre-kindergarten through fifth grade. It includes general classrooms; science, computer, and art rooms; a library, cafeteria, gymnasium, and auditorium; and administrative and support spaces.

The site is on the eastern boundary of a residential neighborhood. To the east, across a main thoroughfare, are Fordham University, the New York Botanical Gardens, and the tracks of the commuter railroad to Manhattan, which is visible to the south from the upper floors of the school.

The building is compact and linear to allow the greatest area of open space around the school for playgrounds, to maximize natural light and ventilation, and to maintain security in relation to the surrounding apartment buildings.

The school has two entrances. The principal entrance for students is through a landscaped courtyard from the residential area to the west. A community entrance opens off the main thoroughfare to the east. The principal playground is to the south, adjoining the cafeteria, and a second play area for the smallest children is to the west, adjoining their classrooms.

Each floor is distinguished by an identifying color. The corridors have color-patterned vinyl tile floors and structural glazed facing tile walls that give identity to each of the classrooms.

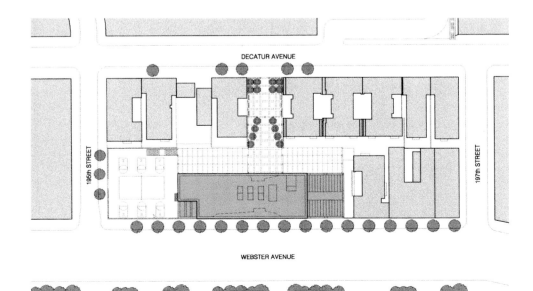

DECATUR AVENUE

195th STREET

197th STREET

WEBSTER AVENUE

2

3

3 View from south
4 East–west sections
5 Upper-floor entrance

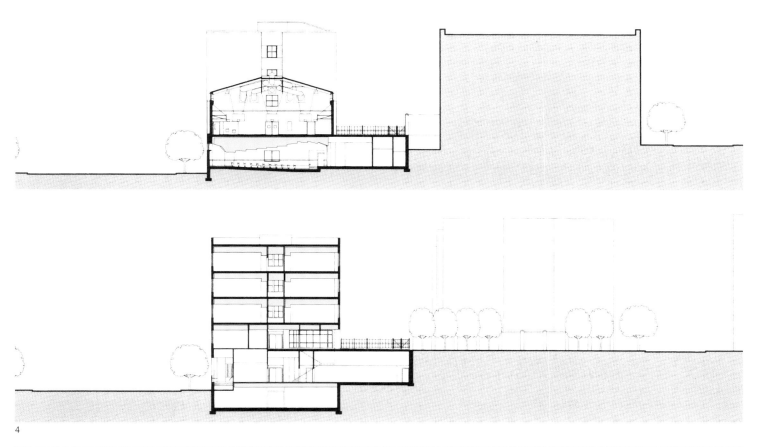

4

5

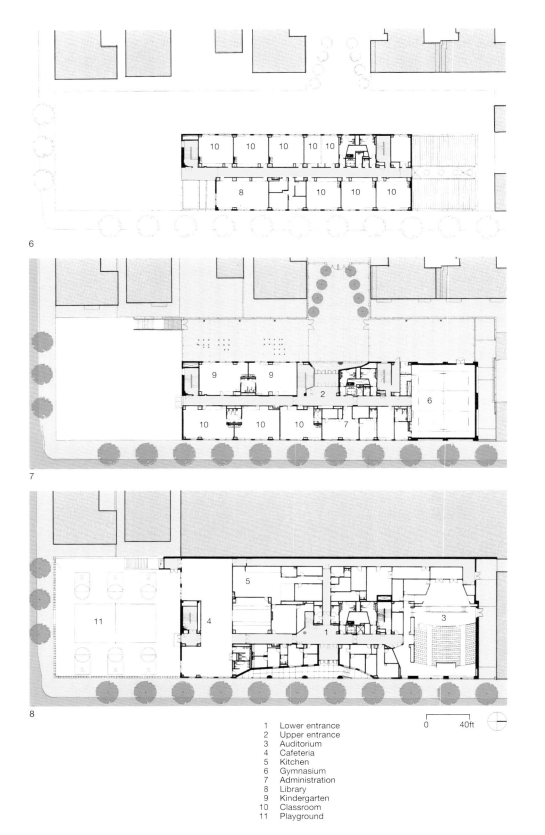

6

7

8

1   Lower entrance
2   Upper entrance
3   Auditorium
4   Cafeteria
5   Kitchen
6   Gymnasium
7   Administration
8   Library
9   Kindergarten
10   Classroom
11   Playground

0   40ft

9

10 Typical corridor detail
11 Lower entrance lobby
12 Upper entrance lobby
13 Typical corridor

10

11

12

13

14

15

Brooklyn, New York

General Services Administration

575,000 square feet

Design 1996/Completion 2003 (Post Office) and 2005 (Courthouse)

Existing load-bearing masonry, steel frame

Painted aluminum and glass window wall, slate roofing, existing granite and terracotta walls, wood windows, custom skylights and laylights, restored plaster and marble walls, wood paneling, plaster ceilings with some decorative painted ceilings, and friezes

U.S. Post Office and Courthouse

This building provides new and renovated space for the U.S. Bankruptcy Court, the U.S. Postal Service, the U.S. Attorney's Office, and the U.S. Trustee.

The original building was completed in 1892 to house Federal Courts and a General Post Office. An extension in matching Romanesque Revival style was built in 1933. Both are on the National Register of Historic Places and are components of the Brooklyn Civic Center. The U.S. Bankruptcy Court, the U.S. Trustee, and their accompanying offices occupy the entire 1892 building, while the 1933 building houses the U.S. Attorney's Office and the U.S. Postal Service. Four courtrooms were restored and four new courtrooms were added to the 1933 building.

The renovation and additions were designed to reinstate the building as a significant presence in the civic life of Brooklyn; to restore historic elements of the existing building; to provide public and judicial spaces that derive their character from the original building; to integrate new elements, spaces, and circulation lightly into the fabric of the existing building; and to introduce natural light throughout.

A new monumental flight of steps connects the entrances to the street and the park. A new 45,000-square-foot mezzanine was constructed over the first floor of the 1933 extension, and 10,000 square feet were added to each of the upper four floors. These provide efficient office space and form a courtyard that opens south to the 1892 building and to the Brooklyn Borough Hall beyond. A new skylight and a new laylight in the atrium of the 1892 building replace the originals, which had been destroyed. The original wood and marble were cleaned and restored, and the paint colors and decorative patterns were replicated.

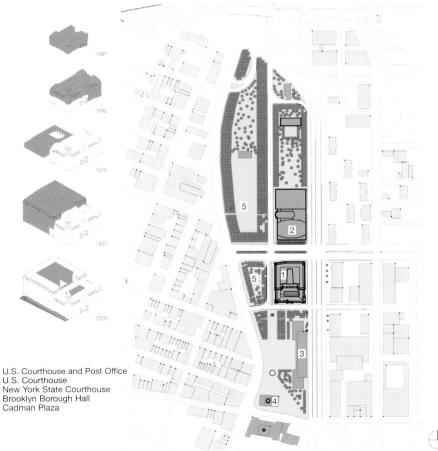

1   U.S. Courthouse and Post Office
2   U.S. Courthouse
3   New York State Courthouse
4   Brooklyn Borough Hall
5   Cadman Plaza

2

Opposite:
    Tower from southwest
2   Site plan

3

4

5

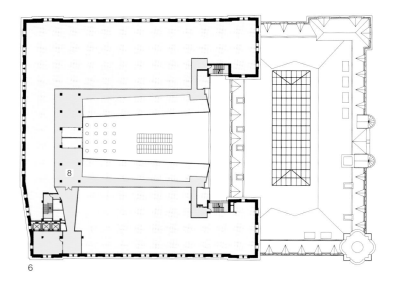

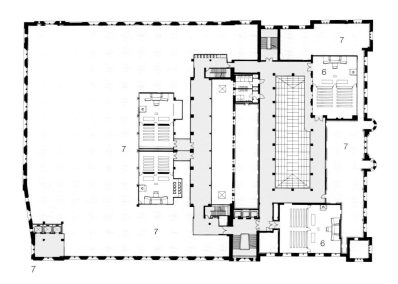

1   Entrance to Bankruptcy Courts
2   Entrance to United States Post Office
3   Entrance to United States Attorney Office
4   Bankruptcy clerk
5   United States Post Office
6   Courtrooms
7   Judges' chambers
8   United States Attorney Offices

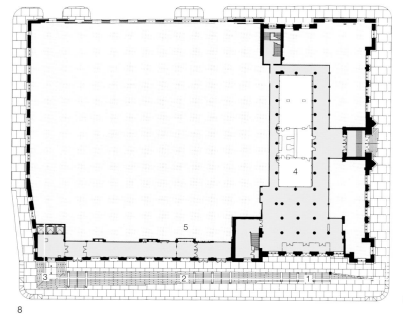

0   50ft

9

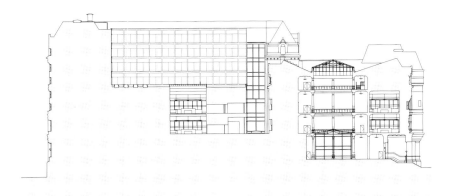

10 North–south section
11 East–west section
12 U.S. Bankruptcy Court entry hall
13 Bankruptcy clerk's intake enclosure

10

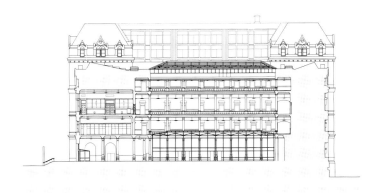

11

12

13

14 Restored historic stair
15 Atrium
16 Atrium from fourth floor

14

15

16

17

18

19

21

23

22   New courtyard view north
23   New courtyard view south

24

25

26

27

25 New courtroom
26&28 Renovated courtroom
27 Skylight in new courtroom

28

1

1 Sterling Divinity Quadrangle and Marquand Chapel
2 Site plan

New Haven, Connecticut

Yale University

135,000 square feet

Feasibility study 1996

Design 1997/Completion 2003

Existing and new concrete foundations, existing load-bearing masonry walls, new steel seismic frames, existing concrete and terracotta cellular floor slabs, new steel floor framing and steel deck with concrete fill, existing steel roof trusses supporting existing concrete roof planks, new steel deck, new HVAC systems

Brick, metal/glass aluminum storefront, custom hollow metal glazed walls, standing seam aluminum roofing and wall panels, slate roofing, EPDM roofing, aluminum monitor clerestory, lead-coated copper flashing and gutters, hollow metal doors, solid-core wood doors, cut bluestone, textured veneer plaster vaulted ceilings, acoustical tile ceiling, painted wallboard, carpet, tile flooring, oak strip flooring, painted pine trim

Yale University, Sterling Divinity Quadrangle

This project is an adaptive reuse of the Sterling Divinity Quadrangle, designed by Delano & Aldrich and completed in 1932. It houses sacred, social, and instructional spaces; a library; and the administrative and faculty offices of the Yale Divinity School, the Institute of Sacred Music, and the Berkeley Divinity School.

The pavilions of the west quadrangle, formerly student residences, have been converted to instructional and administrative uses. They are connected with new enclosures at the second floor by new ramps on the first and second floors. These ramps, along with new elevators, make the entire complex fully accessible. An existing Dean's House and student dormitories have been removed to create a new landscaped oval. Residences for students were relocated to the existing apartment quadrangle on site. A Victorian house on an adjoining site was renovated to provide a residence for the Dean.

In three pavilions of the west quadrangle, portions of the second floors were removed to create double-height spaces for the Institute of Sacred Music's Great Hall and Organ Studio, and a large lecture hall. Other pavilions were renovated to accommodate instructional and common spaces, offices, seminar rooms, and classrooms. The library was reorganized and renovated. The chapel was renovated to provide new lighting, wood floors, and flexible seating that replaced fixed pews. The existing choir loft was expanded for a new organ that was under construction at the time. The reading room and library rotunda were restored and a new porch was added to the north, which marks the principal entrance to the complex.

Three of the four pavilions east of the chapel were not required for the Yale Divinity School program. They were stabilized, and their exterior rehabilitation was completed in anticipation of the growth of school-related programs.

This adaptive reuse was a multi-phased process that enabled the school to remain completely operational throughout construction.

1 Yale Sterling Divinity School campus
2 Yale campus
3 New Haven Green

2

3

4

5

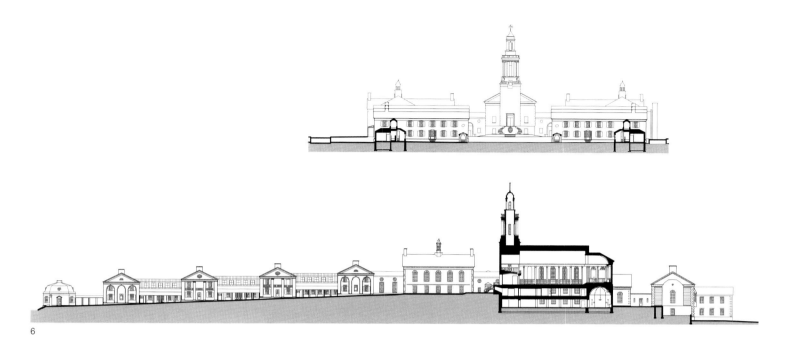

6

7

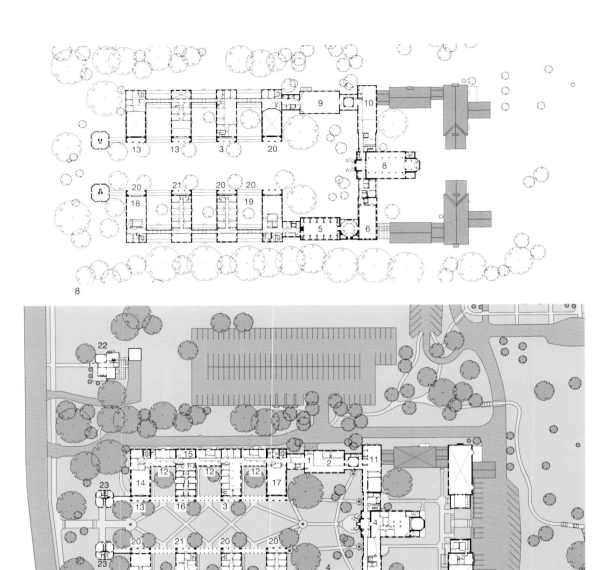

8

9

1   Entrance
2   Bookstore
3   Administration
4   Divinity School Library
5   Library: Day Missions Reading Room
6   Library: Trowbridge Reference Room
7   Library: Ministry Resource Center
8   Marquand Chapel
9   Common room
10   Refectory
11   Commuter lounge
12   Connector lounge
13   Institute of Sacred Music
14   Institute of Sacred Music: Great Hall
15   Institute of Sacred Music: Organ studio
16   Institute of Sacred Music: Practice modules
17   Niebuhr Hall
18   RSV (Revised Standard Version) Room
19   Latourette classroom
20   Offices and instructional
21   Berkley Divinity School
22   Dean's House
23   Stabilized/future renovation

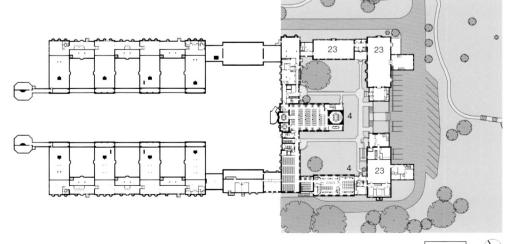

10

0   50ft

12

13

14

15

16

15   Large lecture hall
16   Small lecture hall

17

17 Library reading room, restored
18 Library rotunda, restored

18

19 Connector at lower level
20 Performance hall
21 Common room

19

20

21

1

New York, New York
Columbia University
2100 square feet
Design 1997/Completion 2001
Existing steel frame, terracotta flat-arch slab
Ceramic panels, steel and glass partitions, perforated metal
acoustical panels, painted plaster

Columbia University
Undergraduate Life Sciences Laboratory

The purpose of this renovation was the creation of a modern laboratory facility that also carries forward the historical significance of its space. Room 922, identified as a teaching laboratory on the original McKim, Mead, & White drawings for Schermerhorn Hall from the early 1900s, was the laboratory in which Thomas Hunt Morgan's Nobel Prize-winning research on fruit fly genetics was first conducted.

The project has five components: the main laboratory; a project laboratory; the instructor's office and a teaching assistant room/library; and storage. The main laboratory accommodates up to 32 students per section. The workstations are grouped into three tables of 10, permitting the instructor's office and teaching assistant's room to be located within the volume of the main laboratory.

The original door to the main laboratory is incorporated into a new glazed wall. The ceiling is raised at the eastern edge of the room to incorporate the window of the attic pediment into the space of the laboratory.

The project laboratory occupies what remains of the original Thomas Hunt Morgan laboratory, and is designed to include certain historic references, including equipment and cabinetwork. Some items of equipment that serve the main laboratory, such as incubators, are housed here.

1 Laboratory
2 Site plan

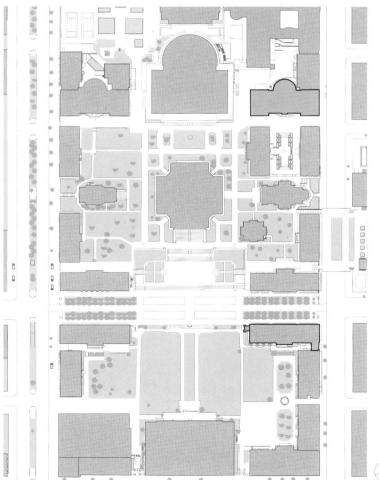

2

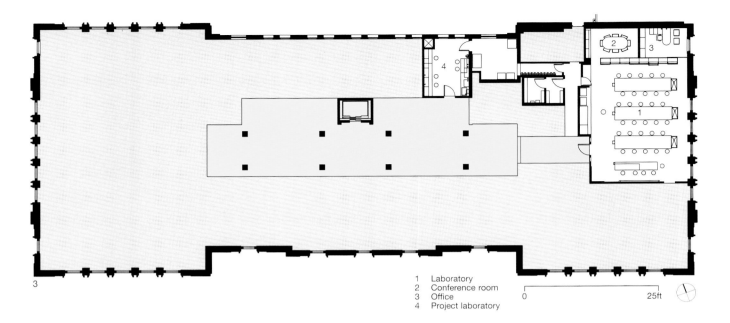

1	Laboratory
2	Conference room
3	Office
4	Project laboratory

0   25ft

3

3   Floor plan
4   Laboratory
5   Laboratory detail
6   Laboratory entrance
7   Interior elevations

4

5

6

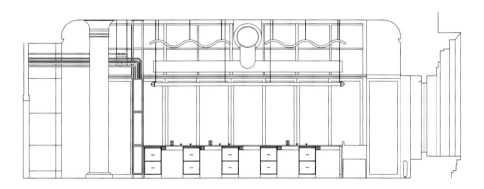

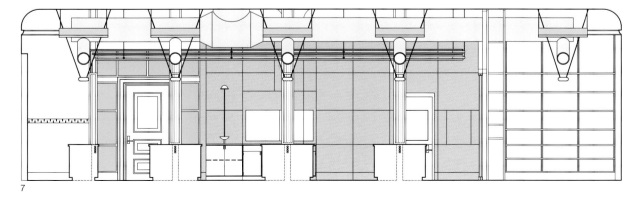

7

New York, New York

New York University

70,100 square feet

Design 1997/Completion 2002 (phase 1); 2005 (phase 2); 2006 (phase 3)

Load-bearing brick masonry walls, cast iron columns, wood joists and wood deck on steel girders

Brick masonry, limestone cladding, steel and glass storefront, curved steel and glass wall, ash veneer doors, granite pavers, ash wood wall paneling, stainless-steel wire-mesh suspended ceiling canopies and wall panels, oak wood floor, fabric-covered acoustic wall panels, custom light fixtures, metal shelving, painted gypsum wallboard ceilings, suspended lay-in acoustic-tile ceilings

New York University
Languages and Literature Building

The renovation of the Languages and Literature Building provides updated facilities for the English, Creative Writing, Languages, and Comparative Literature departments. It includes a new entrance lobby, lecture halls, a computer classroom, and lounges on the ground floor. Seminar rooms and offices for faculty and students are on the upper floors.

The original building was designed in 1904 as the Merck laboratory headquarters. The historic masonry exterior was preserved and new ground-floor entrances were added. Commercial storefronts were replaced with steel and glass entrances and window bays.

Painted steel decorated panels in the new shop fronts relate to the historic cast iron façades in the neighborhood. The interior renovations include the design of a new core, elevators, a mechanical and electrical system, and the reconfiguration of circulation to provide functional and flexible space for individual academic departments.

The ground-floor gathering spaces are designed to open the building to the street. An open stair connects the street level with the basement and second-floor common spaces. The new ground-floor screening room, with a curved wall that defines a gallery space visible from the street, accommodates 135 people. A mural has been commissioned for this wall.

Typical departmental floors are organized to maximize the number of offices with exterior windows. Interiors also receive natural light through clerestories and borrowed lights while graduate-student lounge spaces are located at the ends of the corridors, overlooking the street.

Opposite:
Exterior
2 Site plan

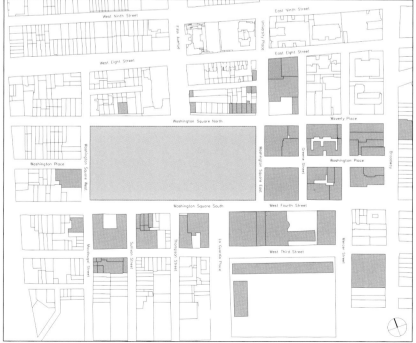

2

3

4

5

3 Gallery
4 Lobby entrance
5 Lobby

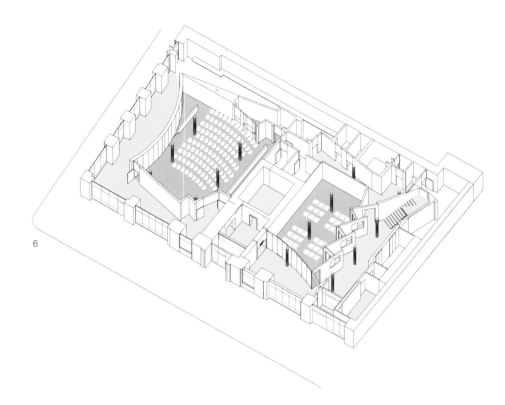

6 Axonometric of ground floor
7&8 Lobby

7

9

9&10   Theater

10

11

11 Classroom
12 Typical office
13 Typical upper-floor plan
14 Upper-floor reception area

12

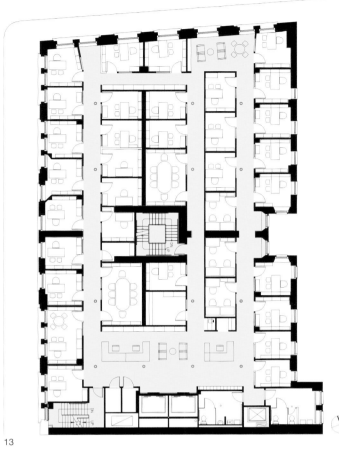

13

14

1

2

3

4

1 Café
2 Conference room
3 Typical office
4 Entry with mailboxes
5 Axonometric
6 Floor plan

Stamford, Connecticut
International Management Consulting Firm
14,000 square feet
Design 1998/Completion 1999
Existing steel frame, concrete-filled metal deck
Steel and glass wall, room-sized sliding whiteboards, sliding glass
doors, painted wallboard, cork flooring, perforated metal ceiling

International Management Consulting Firm Business Technology Office

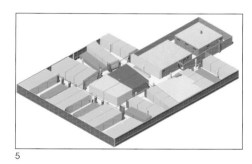

5

This is a prototype office to test design concepts for a Business Technology Consulting Office, a new activity of a worldwide management consulting firm. There are three design goals for the project: the creation of individually controlled workspaces; the creation of flexible group workspaces; and the development of an overall plan that encourages informal interaction and communication.

The office is organized around a central spine, which provides a single populated zone, filled with activity. Support staff are located along the circulation spine in open workspaces. All team rooms, printers, and file banks are located along this central collector, fostering community around shared facilities.

Individual consultants' workspaces are ergonomically designed, and lighting and air conditioning are individually controlled.

Floor-to-ceiling sliding whiteboards provide "play space" to encourage creative thinking and problem solving.

Manufactured furniture components maximize flexibility for future reconfiguration or relocation. Team rooms and a large conference room provide space for formal meetings. The central space with its coffee bar, internet connections, magazine racks, mailboxes, and televisions encourages informal meetings. This daylit "piazza" extends 100 feet through the entire width of the office. Sliding glass doors engage the conference room with the piazza and encourage informal use of this space when not in use for meetings.

The spaces derive special character from the exposed cable trays, which provide visible evidence of the importance of electronic networking in this office community. Sliding glass walls allow visual access and promote flexibility within the community.

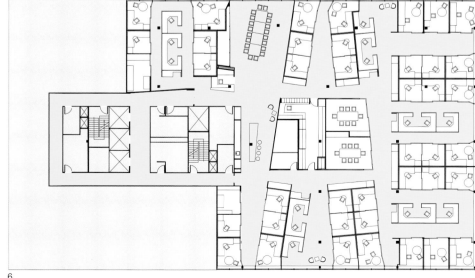

6

New York, New York
Columbia University
70,755 square feet
Design 1998/Completion 2004
Existing steel frame, terracotta flat-arch slab
Granite cladding panels, bronze and glass storefront, custom light fixtures,
bronze railing, marble pavers, oak paneling, plaster walls and ceiling

Columbia University, Hamilton Hall

Hamilton Hall was built in 1905 as the home of Columbia College. Over the years, the building had been transformed to accommodate additional classrooms and offices. This project recaptures the clarity of the original McKim, Mead & White plan, while accommodating current needs.

The ground-floor entrance lobby was restored to the original McKim, Mead & White design, and later additions were removed. New marble floors and lighting fixtures re-create the originals. Two historic monumental Tiffany stained-glass windows, removed from another campus building and stored on campus, were restored and reinstalled in the lobby.

The Admissions Office on the first floor has a new glass pavilion entrance that opens directly onto College Walk. This glass pavilion, inserted within a granite garden wall, opens to South Field and the dormitories, library, and student center that define it. Admissions offices are enclosed in sliding glass walls, which encourage flexible reorganization of the space for a variety of seasonal Admissions Office functions.

Renovations to the 39 classrooms, seminar rooms, and lecture rooms on the upper floors provide access to electronic media, improved lighting, acoustics, and environmental controls. The historic character of the original rooms is maintained by the restored finishes, new oak paneling, and new furniture. The Dean's Office, the Center for the Core Curriculum—with a multimedia conference room—the archives, and the reference library are new spaces with oak paneling designed in the spirit of McKim, Mead & White.

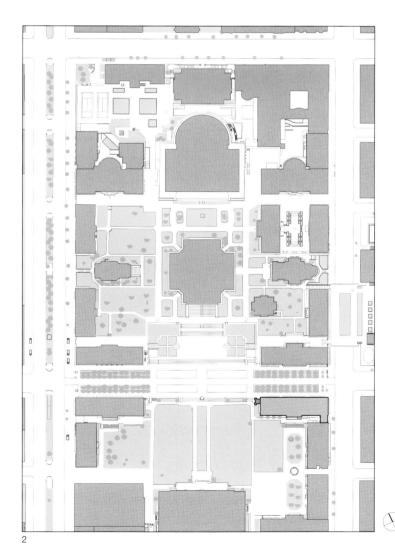

1   New entrance to Admissions Office
2   Site plan

2

3   View from southwest
4&5 New entrance to Admissions Office

3

4

5

6

6   Renovated lobby
7   Restored Tiffany stained-glass window

7

1 Entrance pavilion
2 Admissions Office
3 Dean's office
4 Lobby
5 Center for the Core Curriculum
6 Classroom
7 Faculty office

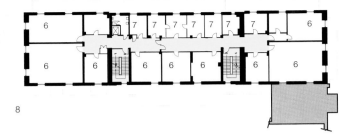

8

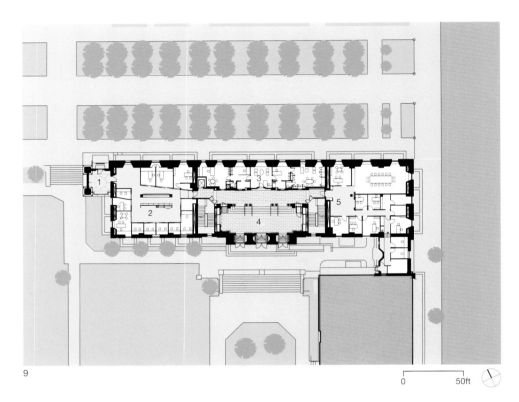

9

0   50ft

8   Typical upper-floor plan
9   Ground-floor plan
10,12&13 Admissions Office
11   Renovated classroom

10

11

12

13

1 View from east with The Cloisters
  museum in the background
2 Aerial view

1

New York, New York
New York City Board of Education
55,000 square feet
Design 1999/Completion 2001
In association with Dattner Architects
Steel frame, concrete-filled metal deck
CMU cavity wall, brick, vinyl tile floors, structural glazed facing tile walls, vinyl mesh

Primary School 178

The new school accommodates 450 students in pre-kindergarten through second grade. It includes general classrooms, science and art rooms, a library, cafeteria, gymnasium, and administrative and support spaces.

The site is in Manhattan in a neighborhood of six- and seven-story apartment buildings, with views of The Cloisters museum. The building is composed of a five-story classroom block and a single-story extension, which houses the cafeteria and kitchen, and a play area on the roof. The gymnasium is located at the east end of the top floor, and has clerestory windows on all sides.

The building is clad in brick. It is designed to relate to, but be distinct from, the neighboring buildings. The street walls on the north and east are light brown with a darker pattern at the ground floor. The walls at the south and west property lines resemble the common red brick of the adjacent party walls. The west walls of the classroom block, however, are white brick to reflect more light onto the roof-top play area, which is protected by dark green vinyl-covered mesh.

The corridors have vinyl tile floors and structural glazed facing tile walls. Each floor is distinguished by an identifying color, and each classroom by a patterned structural glazed facing tile doorway and corresponding vinyl tile "doormat," which give identity to each of the classrooms.

2

3 Gymnasium
4 Section
5 Entrance lobby
6 Top to bottom: fifth-, second-, and first-floor plans
7 View from north
8 Roof playground
9 View from south

3

5

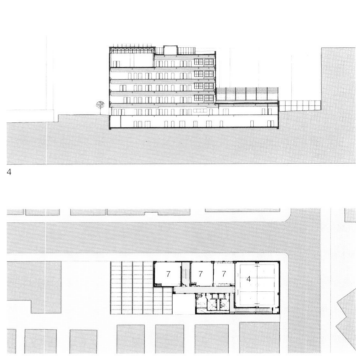

4

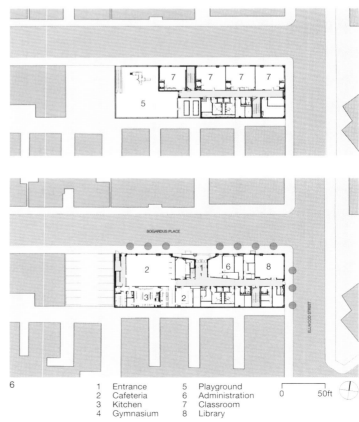

6

1	Entrance	5	Playground
2	Cafeteria	6	Administration
3	Kitchen	7	Classroom
4	Gymnasium	8	Library

0   50ft

7

8

9

1

Albany, New York

State University Construction Fund

76,100 square feet

Design 1999/Completion 2002

Existing poured-in-place and precast concrete system throughout

Precast trims, fabric wallcovering, painted wallboard, terrazzo flooring, carpet, hollow metal, new lighting, new storefront

State University of New York at Albany College of Arts and Sciences Building

Designed by Edward Durell Stone in 1968, the existing building is part of a monolithic single-structure campus. Thirteen academic buildings are connected by a network of continuous three-story colonnades, sitting on a podium containing lecture halls, classrooms, and laboratories. This project, the first major renovation of these buildings, provides a new home for the College of Arts and Sciences. It is both a restoration to the original design intent and a transformation of the building for current needs.

The project includes a new glazed pyramidal entrance to public spaces on the lower podium level, and a complete reorganization of the three-story building that simplifies circulation and introduces daylight into every space.

The new glazed pyramid entrance marks an important node in the campus circulation system, at the intersection of the podium axes and the parking entrance drive. The new pyramid rises 25 feet above the podium level. It brings light into the lower level and incorporates stairs, air intakes, and exhausts for air-handling units.

Building circulation is organized as a simple loop, with perimeter offices and interior support spaces. New glazed walls bring light through the fire stairs and department offices to social spaces at the center of the building. The original precast concrete vaults are exposed and used as light reflectors, with new direct–indirect fluorescent fixtures mounted at the spring point of the barrel vaults. Clerestories bring light into all corridors and borrowed lights illuminate the interior graduate student offices and support spaces. Every occupied space has natural light.

1   Entrance pyramid
2   Site plan

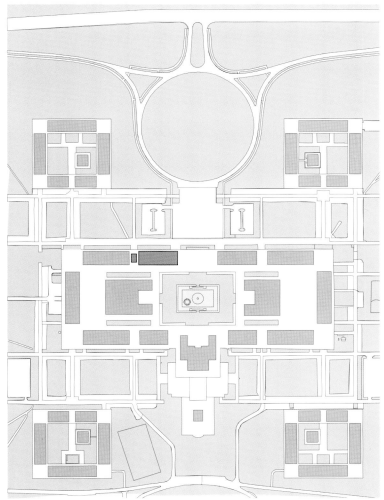

0   200ft

2

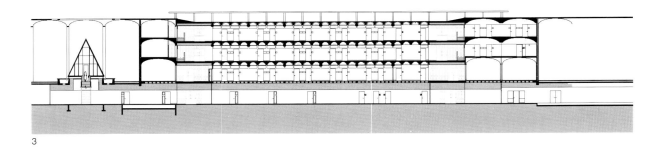

3

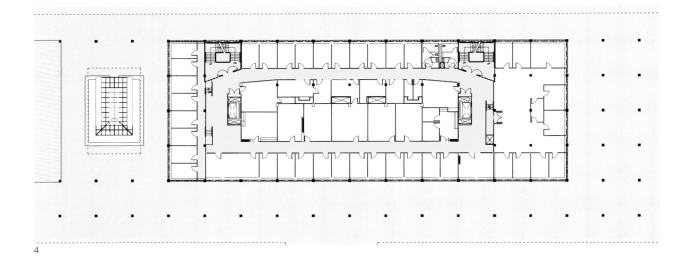

4

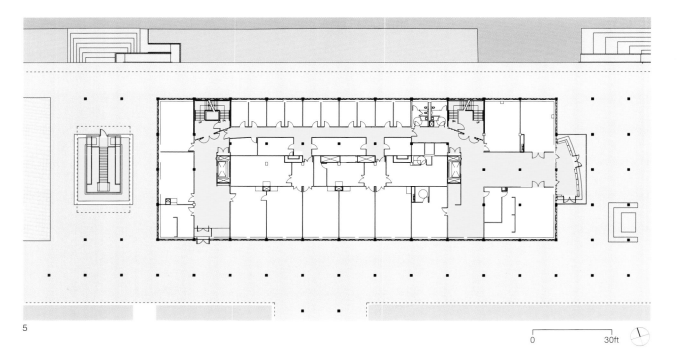

5

0   30ft

6

7

8

1 View from southwest
2 View from south

1

Gulfport, Mississippi
General Services Administration
217,000 square feet
Design 1999/Completion 2003
Cast-in-place concrete columns, beams and wide module waffle-floor slabs
Precast concrete wall panels, granite plinth, bluestone pavers, curtain wall, terrazzo floors and stair, gypsum wallboard, marble panels, pecan and mahogany millwork, acoustical wall panels, carpet on raised access flooring

Dan M. Russell, Jr. United States Courthouse

A new courthouse, a renovated high school, and their related landscapes form a courts complex in the central business district of Gulfport. On axis with a public park and overlooking the Mississippi Sound, the complex includes eight courtrooms: four district, two magistrate, and two bankruptcy with related chambers and support spaces, and a suite for an appellate court judge. It also includes office space for the U.S. Marshals, U.S. Senate, U.S. Attorney, and U.S. Probation.

The new courthouse tower is eight stories with a two-story entrance pavilion. Five-story bay windows mark significant components of the judicial process: public courts waiting areas; judges' chambers; and jury deliberation rooms. At night these bay windows, along with the skylights that bring natural light into the top floor courtrooms during the day, serve to make the courthouse an illuminated beacon, visible from miles around.

The former 1920s Gulfport High School on the site, a National Register of Historic Places landmark, was renovated and adapted for court-related functions. It now accommodates U.S. Attorney and U.S. Probation offices. A new landscaped courtyard at the center of the building is visible from surrounding offices, and provides an amenity shared by the entire courthouse community.

The new courts complex expresses the civic dignity and importance of the judicial process, engages the surrounding community, and extends the history and culture of the place.

2

3

1 Courthouse square
2 Courthouse, new construction
3 Former high school, renovation
4 Service building, new construction

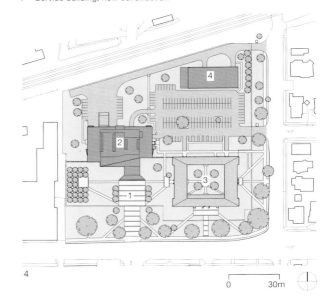

4

0   30m

5

6

3&4 Site plan
   5 View from west
   6 Entrance plaza from west
   7 Entrance from east

7

Dan M. Russell, Jr. United States Courthouse **93**

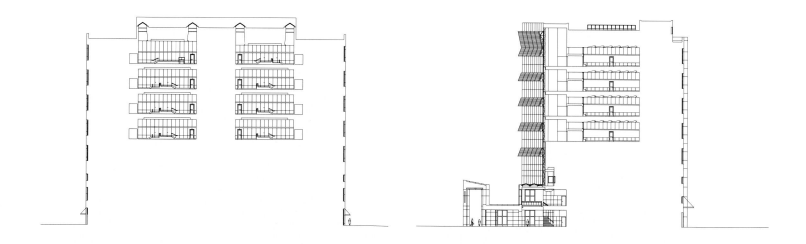

9

10

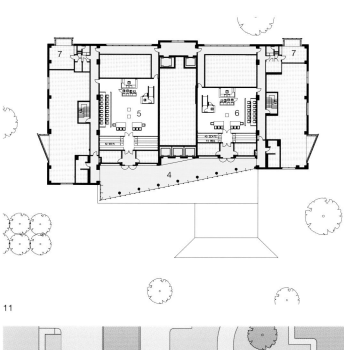

Opposite:
    Courthouse lobby
9   Section looking north
10 Section looking west
11 Public courts floor plan
12 Ground-floor plan

11

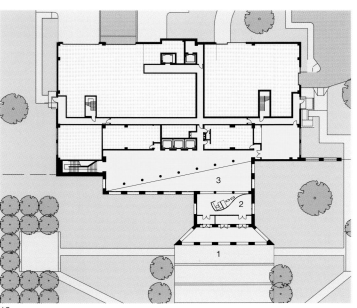

1   Entrance
2   Security screening area
3   Lobby
4   Public courts waiting area
5   District courtroom
6   Magistrate and bankruptcy courtroom
7   Jury deliberation

13

14

15

16

17 Security screen at entrance, designed in
   collaboration with Michele Oka Doner
18 Public courts waiting area, eighth floor
19 Lobby
Following pages:
   Courtroom, eighth floor

17

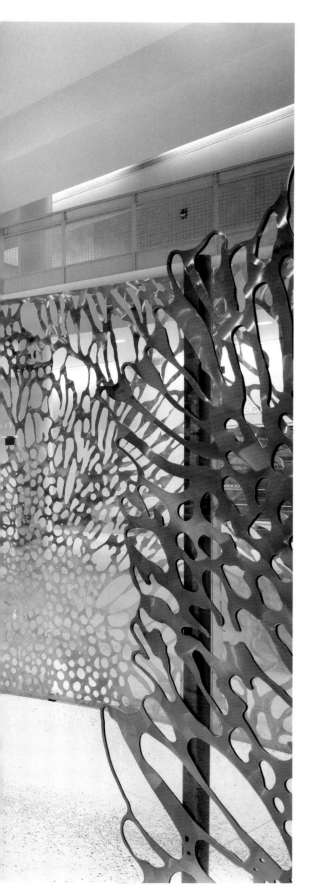

18

19

21

22

23

21 Courtroom, eighth floor
22 District Judges' chambers
23 Jury deliberation room

1

Lancaster, Pennsylvania
Franklin & Marshall College
42,500 square feet
Competition 2000/Completion 2003
Concrete foundation walls with steel frame and CMU infill, concrete-filled metal deck, exposed steel bow trusses
Metal and glass curtain wall, brick, metal panels, cast stone sills, white ceramic fritted glass, aluminum coping, steel barrel-vaulted roof, floated basket-weave floor, custom wood rail, beech veneer panels

Franklin & Marshall College
Roschel Performing Arts Center

The Roschel Performing Arts Center is the new home of the Department of Theater, Dance, and Film. A new wing houses a 305-seat theater, lobby, scene shop, and mechanical spaces and is joined to an existing building—a former swimming pool—renovated into dance studios, classrooms, a costume shop, a video production room, and miscellaneous back-of-house functions.

The Performing Arts Center joins the music center, the student center, and the Phillips Museum of Art to define a landscaped plaza that is open to the life of the community. At the plaza entrance to the Performing Arts Center, a new terrace is shared with the student center café.

The defining elements of the new wing are a curved arcade that connects the renovated dance studios to the student center, and the rectangular, barrel-vaulted enclosure of the theater. Between them, a skylit lobby overlooks the plaza and serves the buildings around it. The arcade is made of brick and cast stone, with painted aluminum windows. The theater is faced with beech paneling in the lobby, and painted aluminum paneling above the lobby roof.

The theater is designed for optimum flexibility and accessibility: there are catwalks above the seating and the stage; the clerestory windows can be blacked out; the orchestra pit can be converted to a thrust stage; and the scene shop adjoins the stage and has direct access to the loading area and service drive.

The dance studios in the renovated former pool building take advantage of the high ceilings and large windows to provide airy, naturally lit spaces.

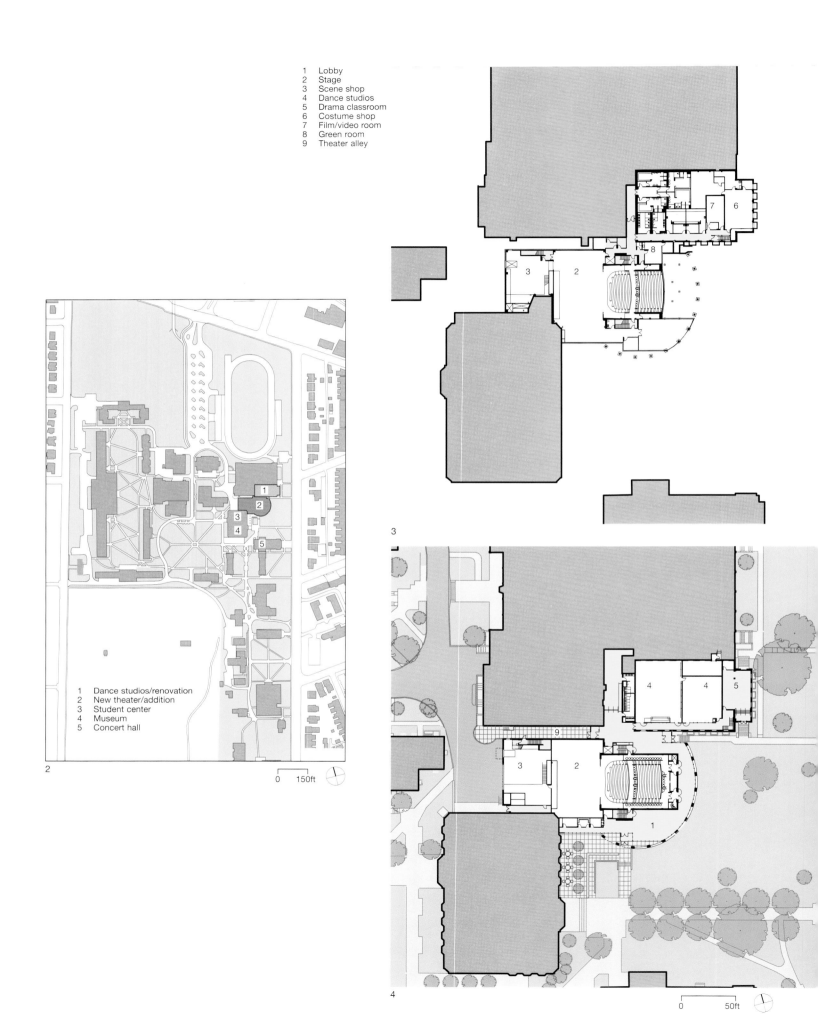

1 Lobby
2 Stage
3 Scene shop
4 Dance studios
5 Drama classroom
6 Costume shop
7 Film/video room
8 Green room
9 Theater alley

1 Dance studios/renovation
2 New theater/addition
3 Student center
4 Museum
5 Concert hall

2

0   150ft

3

4

0   50ft

5

6

7

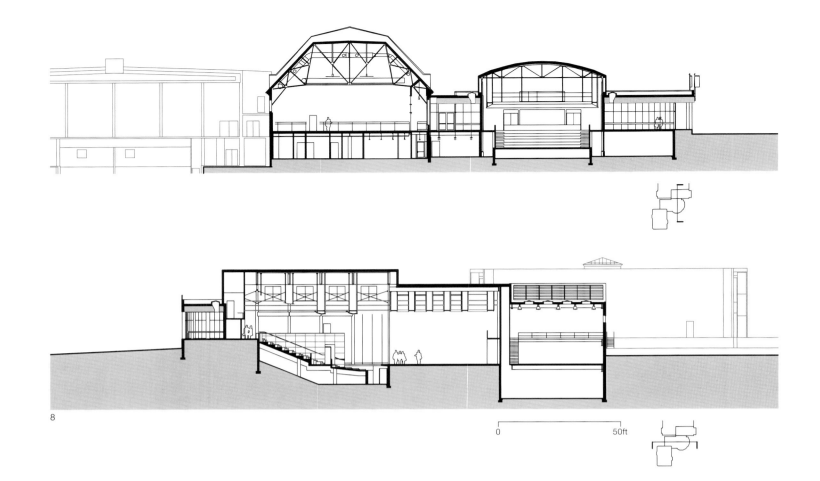

8

0   50ft

9

8   Sections
9   Dance studio
10 Theater lobby
11 Theater
12 View from lobby level seating
13 Catwalk

10

11

12

13

1

2

Glenside, Pennsylvania
Arcadia University
50,000 square feet
Competition 2000/Completion 2003
Concrete foundation walls with steel frame and CMU infill, concrete-filled metal deck, exposed steel "tree" columns in main reading room
Limestone and granite façade panels, aluminum-frame curtain wall, precast concrete, single-ply EPDM roofing, mahogany-frame windows at limestone façade, aluminum-frame windows at curtain wall, beech-veneer panels, beech-veneer bookcases, circulation, and reference desks, bluestone paving, painted steel-and-glass stair enclosure, carpet

Arcadia University, Landman Library

The expanded library accommodates 150,000 volumes, a multimedia collection, the college archive, a curriculum library for the education program, study seating for 300 students in reading rooms, group study rooms, individual carrels, multimedia classrooms, and the boardroom for the Board of Trustees.

The new wing sits at the south face of the existing library. It completes the central campus, forming a quadrangle with the historic Grey Towers Castle, student dormitories, and academic buildings. It also defines a series of outdoor spaces to the east and west.

The curved limestone of the library's south elevation forms a memorable campus landmark and is a distinctive presence at the heart of the campus. The wall defines the north edge of the central quadrangle, a soccer field, and the campus green.

The design of the library enhances the reader's experience by providing many different spaces for reading and study, with access to controlled daylight and campus views. A two-story-high reading room on the second floor extends the full width of the building and looks out over the green to the castle. Daylight enters through monumental wood windows with adjustable sunscreens and shutters, and high clerestory windows bring light in from the north.

The ground-floor reference room also extends the full width of the building, and includes the reference collection, exhibit space, circulation desk, and computer workstations. The periodical lounge is a two-story-high glazed space facing north to a garden and west to a grove of beech trees.

The circulating collection is housed on three floors in reconfigured, accessible stacks in the older portion of the building, adjacent to study and faculty carrels, group study rooms, and a small café.

1   View from south at dusk
2   View from south
Following pages:
    Entrance portico

4 Northeast corner of addition
5 Site plan
6 Periodical reading room
Following pages:
  View from southwest

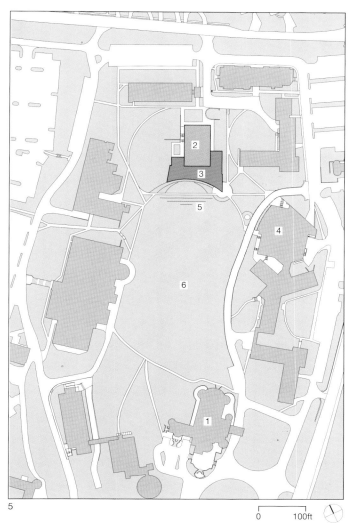

5

0   100ft

1 Grey Towers Castle
2 Library, renovation
3 Library, new construction
4 Dining hall
5 Library reflection lawn
6 Campus green

6

8

9

1	Reference room
2	Periodical reading room
3	Main reading room
4	Computer lab

10

11

1	Reference room
2	Periodical reading room
3	Curriculum library
4	Reference alcove
5	Work room
6	Circulation desk

0   50ft

12　Periodical reading room

13

14

15

16

1

2

Hyde Park, New York
National Archives and Records Administration
50,800 square feet
Design 2001/Completion 2004
Steel frame, concrete foundation, heavy timber posts, beams, and trusses, exposed steel bow-trusses
Local fieldstone, Western red cedar clapboard and shiplap siding, lead-coated copper, Douglas fir framing and wood decking, beech acoustic panels, ceramic-tile corridors, cedar wood and glass curtain wall, stained wood siding, custom light fixtures

Franklin D. Roosevelt Presidential Library and Museum
Henry A. Wallace Visitor and Education Center

The Henry A. Wallace Visitor and Education Center provides space for visitor orientation to the Presidential Library, the Roosevelt Home, Val-kill, and Top Cottage. It also houses an Education and Conference Center for the Library and the Franklin and Eleanor Roosevelt Institute. Renovations to the historic Library provide a new gallery for temporary exhibitions.

The new Wallace Center is a gateway to the Home of Franklin D. Roosevelt National Historic Site. It is located directly north of the Library.

The building contains a series of pavilions framing a courtyard, which faces toward the Library. The principal public spaces of the visitor center include the orientation lobby, auditorium, gift shop, and café. The education and conference center includes

three multipurpose rooms that can be used for classes, conferences, and banquets. A multimedia conference room is linked to the auditorium and multipurpose room and the complex has satellite uplink capabilities for broadcasting.

The Wallace Center opens onto and shapes adjacent landscapes. The café and multipurpose rooms open onto the courtyard, which is a gathering space for visitors proceeding to the Library, and the conference rooms open toward the neighboring Beatrix Ferrand Garden. New roads and parking are located to provide minimal intrusion on historic vistas and landscapes.

The structure is characterized by wood-framed gable-roofed pavilions, fieldstone walls, and long, covered porches. The materials and forms of the structure are related to those of the Library, which recalls the historic Dutch Colonial architecture of the Hudson Valley.

The buildings and site are designed to achieve LEED certification for sustainability and environmental compatibility.

1   Entrance from west
2   Courtyard from south

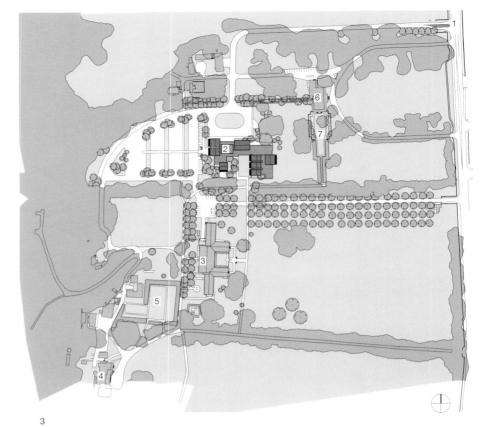

1 New entrance to site
2 Visitor Center
3 Franklin D. Roosevelt Presidential Library
4 Springwood Mansion
5 Rose garden and Franklin D. Roosevelt gravesite
6 Bellefield Mansion
7 Beatrix Ferrand Garden

3

4

5

3 Site plan
4 Principal entrance from north
5 Glass-roofed porches

6 Café
7 Gift shop
8 Courtyard from southeast
9 Sections

6

7

8

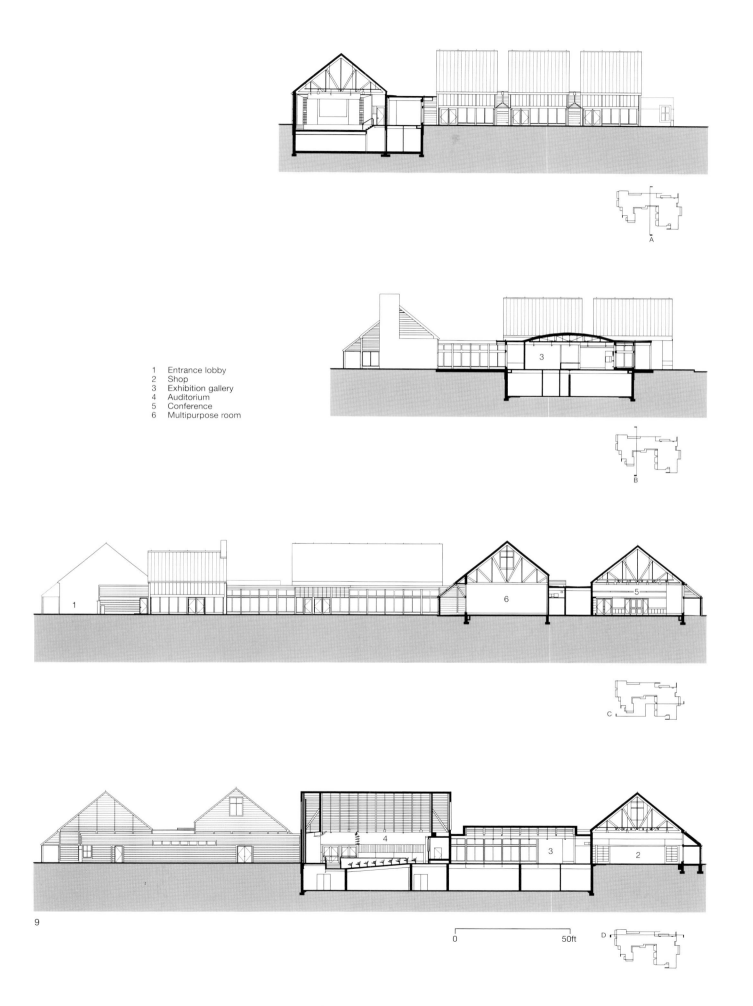

1 Entrance lobby
2 Shop
3 Exhibition gallery
4 Auditorium
5 Conference
6 Multipurpose room

9

0   50ft

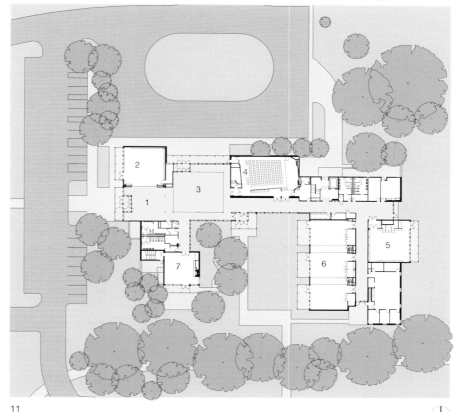

1 Entrance lobby
2 Shop
3 Orientation gallery
4 Auditorium
5 Conference
6 Multipurpose room
7 Café

11

10 Orientation gallery from entrance
11 Floor plan
Following pages:
    Exhibition gallery

To Café & Restrooms

Heritage Area

13

13 Auditorium
14 Conference room
15 Multipurpose room

14

15

Lexington, Kentucky
University of Kentucky
40,250 square feet
Design 2002/Completion 2004
Existing masonry bearing walls with steel joists and composite slabs, steel-framing at walls and roof
Salvaged brick, salvaged stone, cast-stone sills, copings, water table, lead-coated copper standing-seam roof and wall panels, aluminum windows, stainless-steel handrails, precast concrete panels with glass pavers, mahogany panels, mahogany solid running wainscot, red oak flooring, porcelain tile, suspended acoustical ceiling, wood blinds, painted wallboard, storefront glass wall, aluminum perforated metal panels with custom perforated logo, custom skylights

University of Kentucky, Main Building

This project is the reprogramming and reconstruction of the university's Main Building, which had been destroyed by fire. Only its masonry bearing walls remained usable. Completed in 1882, the original building was the center of a new college campus. The campus has since grown into a large research university, leaving the Main Building peripheral in location and significance. By means of its program and design, this project re-establishes the building as the administrative and symbolic heart of the expanding campus.

The building houses the offices of the President, Provost, senior administrators and staff, meeting rooms, classrooms, and the university visitor center. New stairs and services have been placed for the most effective utilization of the restored masonry enclosure. The visitor center and "smart" classrooms on the ground floor are accessible from the new campus entrance. The President's and Provost's suites and the double-height public meeting room open onto new porches that face the campus.

The building design makes a clear distinction between the restored historic walls and the new elements. A large limestone coping caps the restored brick and limestone walls at the original cornice line; a new three-level steel porch with inset glass floors opens the building to the campus; the recessed aluminum windows give prominence to the restored masonry walls; and the configuration of the lead-coated copper roof and tower accommodates the new mechanical equipment and reflects the transition between public and campus orientations, giving identity and natural light to the top-floor meeting rooms and central corridor.

The re-graded site makes the new campus entrance easily accessible and the stone-paved plaza and steel porch are gathering places that serve to reconnect the building to the life of the campus.

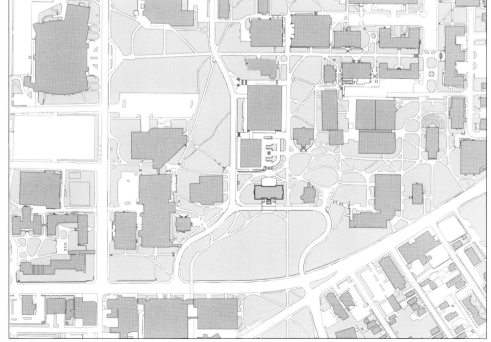

Opposite:
  Front of Main Building at dusk
2 Site plan

2

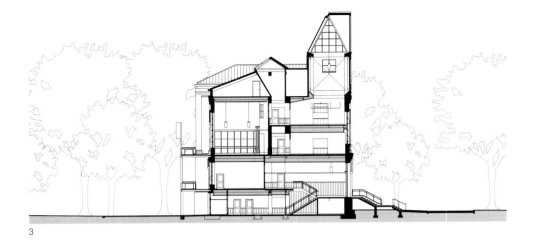

3

4

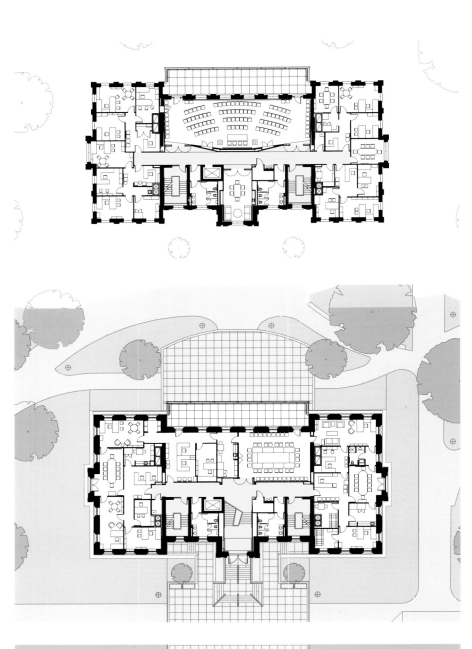

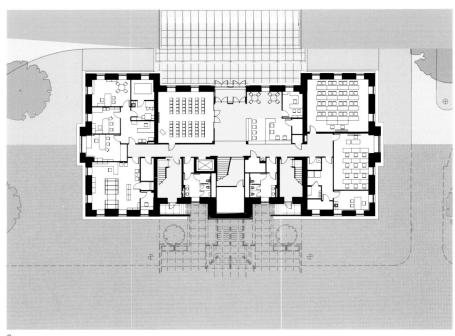

6

7

6 Top to bottom: third-floor plan,
   second-floor plan, first-floor plan
7 Main Building from campus
8 Entry stairs

8

9

10

12

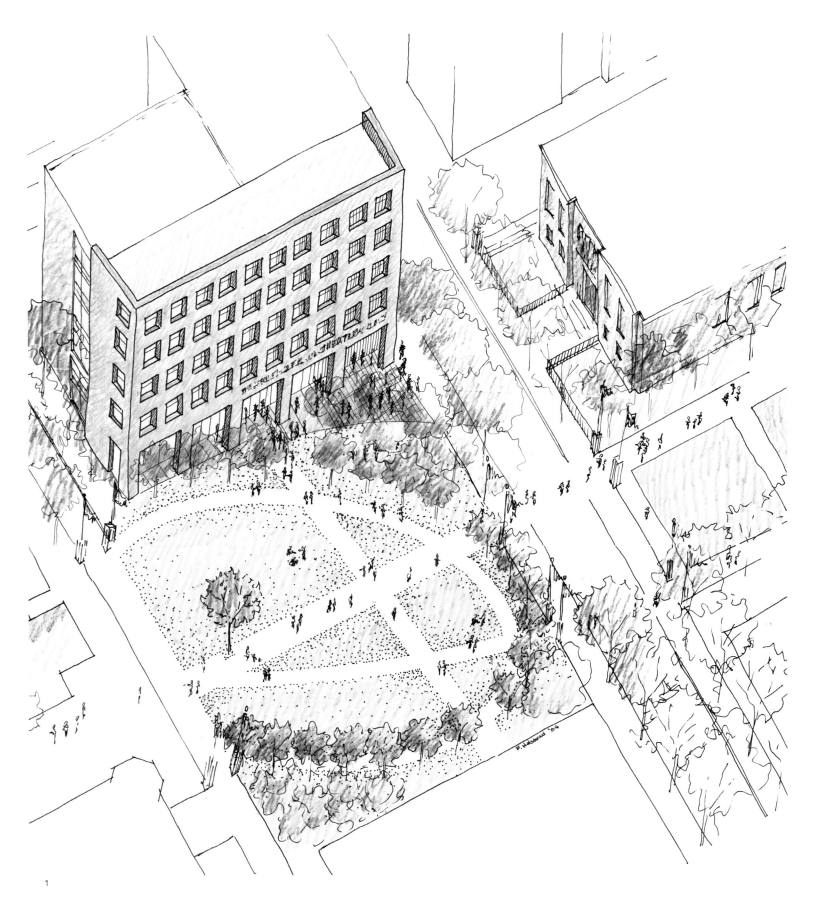

Providence, Rhode Island
Brown University
6,200,000 square feet
Design 2002/Completion 2006–

Brown University
Strategic Framework for Physical Planning

The objective of this study was to develop a plan for future growth in support of the Academic Enrichment Initiatives outlined by the president and approved by the Corporation, while also recognizing the objectives and concerns of the surrounding community.

The 15-month planning process included participation of faculty, students, staff, alumni, parents, elected officials, neighboring businesses and institutions, and community groups. Research and analysis included mapping current use patterns and green space, evaluation of 235 university buildings, and studies of density of use and zoning. A grant from the Getty Center provided further opportunity to study the history of the Brown campus and to make recommendations for the preservation of its extraordinary collection of historic buildings.

Three recommendations emerged: develop circulation infrastructure to foster community; consolidate the historic core campus to increase density and preserve its vitality; and move beyond College Hill in planning for the long-term future. These principles describe a strategy for enhancing the campus environment, making more effective use of existing campus assets, meeting space needs through expansion of facilities on campus and selected acquisitions off campus, and positioning the university for long-term growth.

The plan identified opportunities for one million square feet of infill construction within the present boundaries of the campus and 500,000 square feet of renovations to major structures to make better use of existing assets. The Walk, a new green space linking the Brown and Pembroke campuses, is the locus for several new academic building sites that will strengthen the core. Future growth, including research centers and the medical school, is directed to redevelopment sites in downtown Providence. A shuttle system will link the old and new campus sites.

1&2   The Walk

2

1770

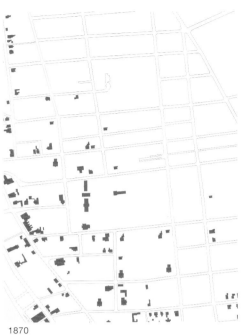

1870

1904

1938

1975

2003

3

3   History of growth
4   Campus plan

4

Blue buildings – renovation
Red buildings – new construction

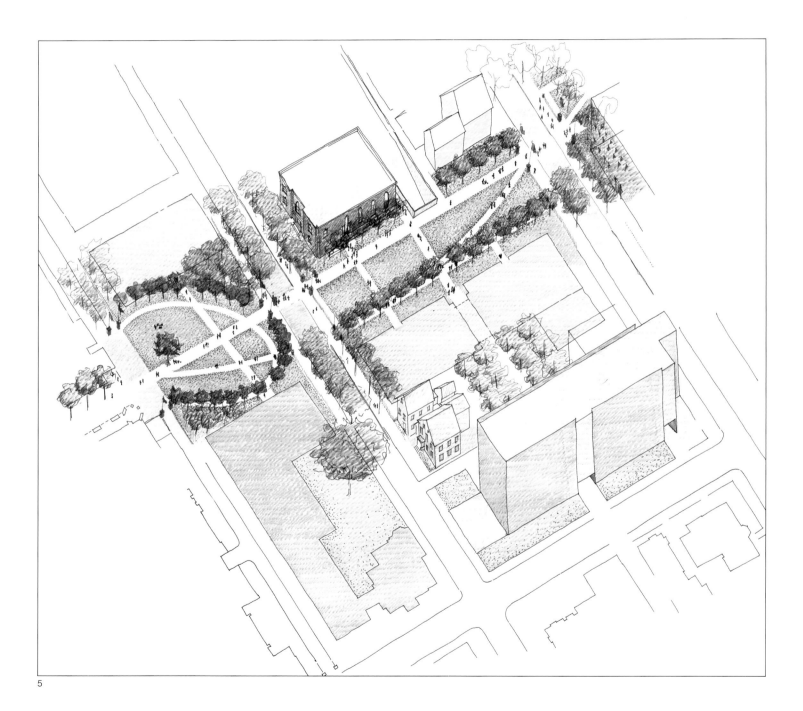

5

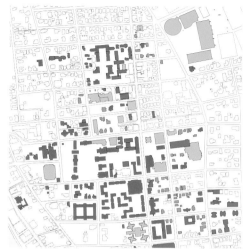

Building evaluation

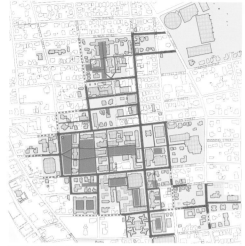

Pedestrian traffic

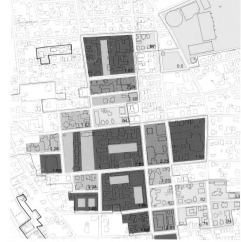

Density evaluation

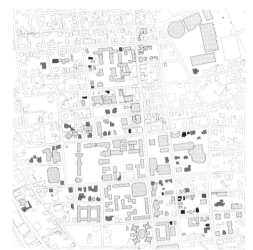

House evaluation

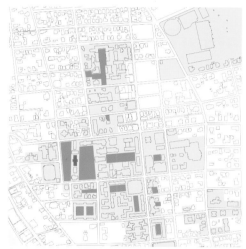

Green space

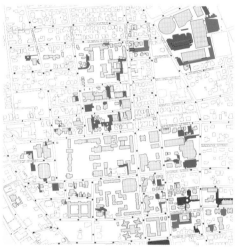

Vehicular circulation and parking

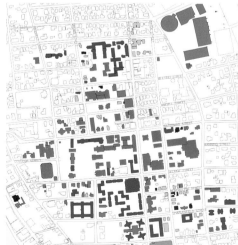

Building use by category

Zoning

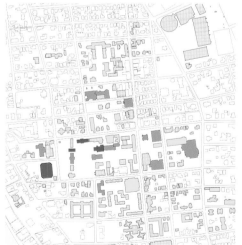

Accessibility

6

1 View from City Hall Park
2 Entrance hall and reception
3 Studio corridor

2

1

New York, New York
Dance New Amsterdam
25,000 square feet
Design 2004/Completion 2006
Existing load-bearing masonry with wood joists
Stainless-steel stairs, painted gypsum wallboard, sprung hardwood
maple flooring, ceramic tile, vinyl tile

Dance New Amsterdam School Studios and Theater

Dance New Amsterdam is a studio school and performance space located in a historic loft building in Lower Manhattan, facing City Hall Park. The studios are designed for ballet, modern, hip-hop and jazz, yoga, and pilates. The performance space includes a wide stage and wing space, and theater seating for 135 people. A gallery, café, dressing rooms, and offices complete the program.

The school has its own storefront entrance, a welcoming place with a café, dance shop, and reception center. An open stair links the reception space to a skylit gallery on the floor above. This gallery atrium is the heart of the school, functioning as an informal gathering space, event space, and theater lobby. It is surrounded by studios, dressing rooms, and school offices. The space is defined by the skylight, and traces of the brick bearing walls of the original structure.

Every dance studio is located to maximize natural light, with south-facing windows opening over City Hall Park, or skylights bringing daylight from above. The skylights form oases of calm and repose within the space.

The studios fit within the structural grid of the building. Original cast-iron columns define each space. The studio corridor borrows light from the studios, with full-height glass windows offering views of the classes within. The corridor is wide enough to serve as an informal warm-up space and viewing gallery for adjacent classes. Saturated colors are used to identify individual studios and important gathering spaces.

3

Opposite:
Stair to studios
5 Ground-floor plan
6 Second-floor plan
7 Studio level lobby

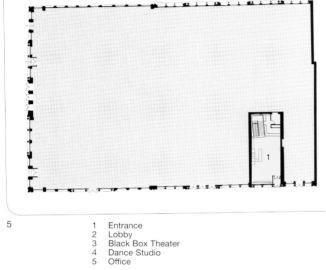

5

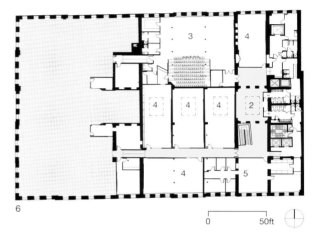

6

0   50ft

1 Entrance
2 Lobby
3 Black Box Theater
4 Dance Studio
5 Office

7

8

9

10

11

8,9&12   Studio
   10   Studio corridor
   11   Studio-level gallery
Following pages:
        Black Box Theater

12

1

2

Brewster, New York

Temple Beth Elohim

26,000 square feet

Design 2003/Completion 2006

Steel frame

Brick, Jerusalem stone, standing seam metal roofing, aluminum windows with metal and wood spandrel panels, exposed steel ceiling joists, wood slat ceilings, white oak wall paneling, folding wall panels, painted gypsum board, white oak flooring, vinyl tile, carpet

Temple Beth Elohim

The new home of the Temple Beth Elohim congregation houses a sanctuary, social hall, library, religious school, and administrative offices. The sanctuary, which uses moveable seating, has a capacity of 300. On the High Holy Days it can seat a maximum of 800 by opening to the social hall and to a temporarily erected tent. Even when expanded, the sanctuary preserves the coherence and the focus of a single space for worship.

Access to the upward-sloping site is via a steep road from the state highway. The site has unobstructed views of distant green hills to the west and south.

The access drive borders the parking lot and leads to a drop-off zone at the columned portico that marks the main entrance. A grove of trees and a lawn shield the classrooms facing the entrance area. Another lawn at the lower level adjoins the classrooms for the younger children. It is connected to the paved courtyard at the main level by means of a berm that also serves as seating overlooking the lawn and the surrounding trees.

The building mass gives expression to the principal elements of the temple: the sanctuary, the social hall, the library, and the school. A courtyard joins these elements to one another and to their natural surroundings. Large windows and high ceilings allow the entire building to be suffused with ample natural light and give a sense of it reaching out to the light.

1   View from access road
2   View from highway
Following pages:
    Sanctuary entrance from northwest

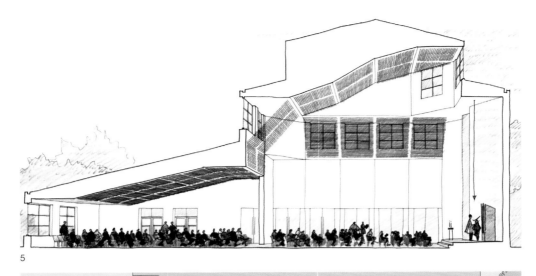

5

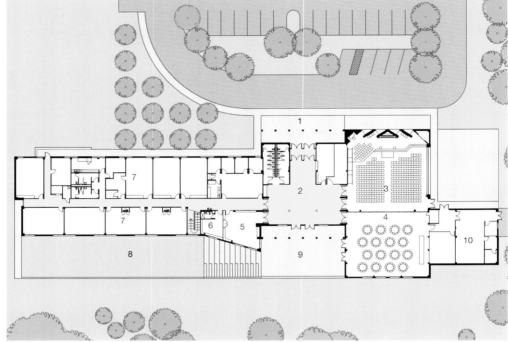

1 Entrance porch
2 Entrance lobby
3 Sanctuary
4 Social hall
5 Library/conference
6 Rabbi study
7 Classrooms
8 Play area
9 Courtyard and porch
10 Kitchen

6

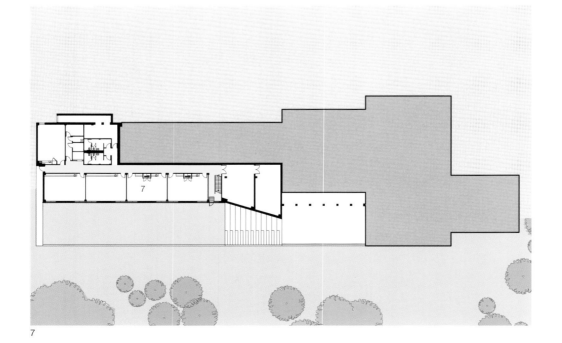

7

8

9

10

11

12

13

13&Opposite:
  Sanctuary

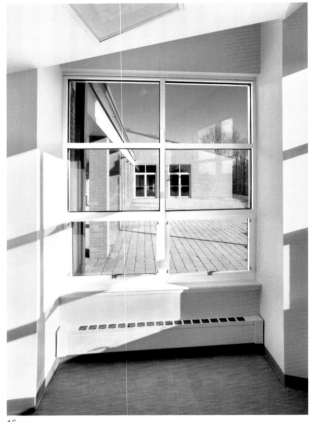

15

17

16

15 View from library to south terrace
16 South terrace
17 Social hall

18 School stair and corridor
19 Classroom
20 Section

19

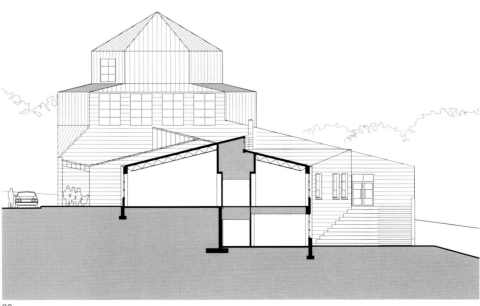

20

1

1   View of plaza from south
2   Aerial view of site

Bronx, New York

New York City Board of Education

145,800 square feet

Design 2004/Scheduled completion 2008

Steel frame, concrete-filled metal deck, CMU cavity wall

Brick, cast-stone trim and copings, aluminum windows, standing seam steel roofing, high-strength wallboard, ground-faced acoustic block, ceramic mosaic tile, stained MDF, wood floor, vinyl tile

Monroe High School Annex

The new Monroe High School Annex will accommodate 1144 students in two identical, but independent schools housed in one building. Each school includes classrooms, art and science rooms, and administrative offices. The two schools share a library, auditorium, gym, cafeteria, music rooms, and the nurse's station. The new building also houses special education facilities.

The site is located adjacent to the existing Monroe High School in the Bronx, in a neighborhood of two- and three-story residential buildings and occasional six- to fifteen-story apartment houses. The entrance to the school is off the street through a landscaped courtyard. From the southeast corner, the site slopes down to the north. The slope allows the portion of the basement floor that houses the cafeteria and kitchen to be exposed to daylight and fully accessible from the exterior.

The massing of the building and the various brick colors and patterns reflect the individuality of the two high schools, the shared auditorium and gym, and the entry courtyard. The five-story block houses the two schools, while the gym and auditorium are separate. The placement of these lower-scale elements between the existing high school and the new school building reinforces the idea of a school campus and helps define the entrance courtyard. It also allows the auditorium to be adjacent to the main entrance and the gym to have direct access to the playing fields.

2

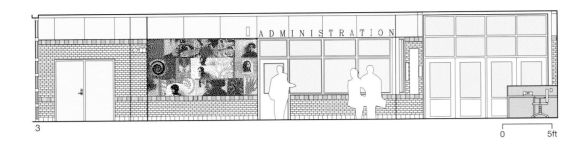

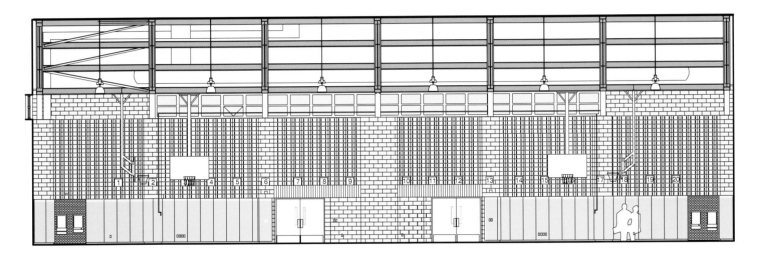

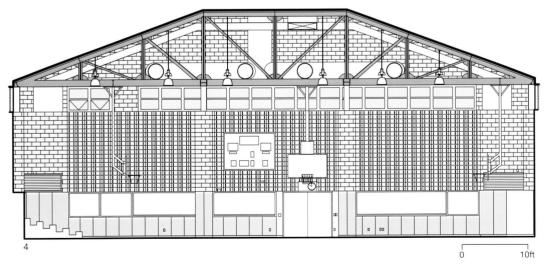

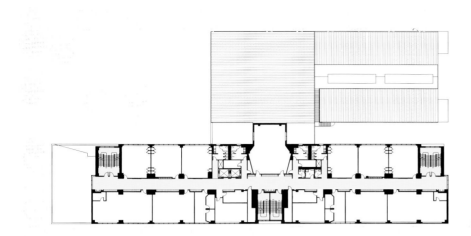

5

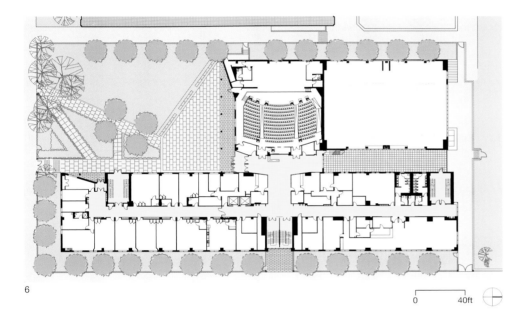

6

0   40ft

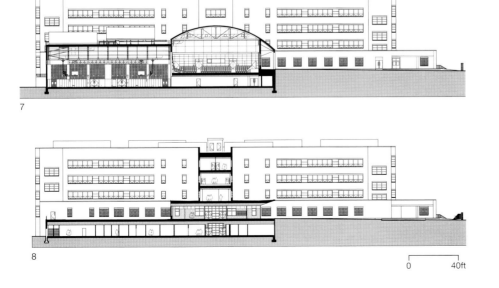

7

8

0   40ft

9

10

11

12

1

New York, New York

Avalon Bay Communities, Inc.

350,000 square feet

Design 2005/Scheduled completion 2008

Cast-in-place concrete columns and floor slabs

Brick, limestone panels, copper trim, metal and glass window panels, wood acoustical wall panels, custom photoglass, MDF panels, rubber flooring, slate, vinyl tile, carpet

Avalon Morningside Park Apartments

This new rental apartment building includes 300 apartments, a fitness center, screening room, 150-car garage, and a two-story lobby and lounge opening onto a landscaped garden. The project, sited on the southeast corner of the Cathedral Close, at the Cathedral of St. John the Divine, will provide revenue for the restoration and mission of the cathedral.

The site, the development guidelines, and the maximum building envelope were defined in consultation with the New York City Landmarks Preservation Commission and the Board of Trustees of the cathedral.

The design of the building relates to both the Cathedral Close and the adjoining Morningside Park. The building aligns with the adjacent cathedral buildings defining the street, and fans open at the corner to views of the park and the city beyond. Warm gray brick on the street wall matches the color of brick and stone of the Cathedral Close. The lower portion of the wall facing onto the close is intricately detailed, with stone string courses and copper trim of a scale that relates to surrounding buildings. Above the fourth floor and facing the park, the metal and glass skin is lighter in color and weight, and reflects the sky.

At the street corner, the building lobby opens onto the garden plaza, which engages Morningside Park across the street. The new plaza is a quiet sitting space in the daytime and an active illuminated corner at night.

1   View from southeast
2   Site plan

2

3

4

3 South elevation
4 View from southeast
5 Typical upper-floor plan
6 Ground-floor plan

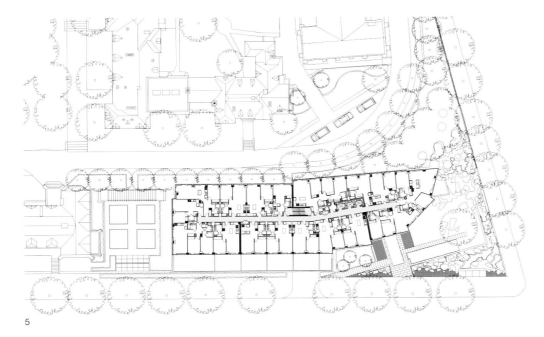

5

1 Entrance
2 Lobby
3 Office
4 Parking garage entrance

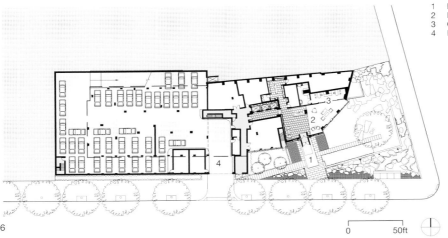

6

0   50ft

7

8

9

7 North elevation
8 View from northwest
9 Street entrance

1

2

New York, New York

American Museum of Natural History

9000 square feet

Design 2006/Scheduled completion 2008

Existing load-bearing masonry, composite slabs and steel roof trusses

Steel framing at mezzanine, painted wallboard, rated glass and steel wall, stainless-steel handrails, restored glass laylight, restored plaster ceilings, restored Minton-tile floor, new cork floor, restored hardwood floor, suspended acoustic ceiling, fabric-wrapped acoustic panels, custom millwork benches and workstations of recycled content sheet material, and custom backlit signage and display case

American Museum of Natural History Graduate and Postdoctoral Center

The Graduate and Postdoctoral Center will house the Museum's new graduate program in comparative biology, the first museum program in the United States to grant PhDs. Occupying the top floor of the historic 1891 Museum building designed by Josiah Cleveland Cady, it will accommodate a student center, a teaching lab, administrative offices, and a 50-person lecture hall.

The project will provide a home base for graduate students now scattered throughout the complex and provide a new 21st-century identity for GPDC within the restored historic fabric of the building. The Graduate Center is located along the "Golden Corridor of Science," the monumentally scaled public corridor that encompasses more than 600 feet of the Museum's upper floor. Sections of the corridor wall will be glazed, bringing in natural light and making the corridor visible from the center.

The elevator lobby will feature new signage and an interactive touch screen describing events, research, and other information for students and visitors.

The heart of the complex is a new student center, a place for collaborative projects, individual research, and group activities. The student center is a double-height space ringed with a new mezzanine that has individual student research spaces. A glass wall joins the main corridor with the student center.

The lecture hall, located in the west turret, will accommodate lectures, seminars, and informal gatherings, with flexible seating for 50 people, improved lighting and acoustics, and video conferencing capabilities. A 25-person teaching lab will support academic programs and serve as break-out space for large seminars and functions held in the lecture hall.

1   View from mezzanine
2   View from south
3   Floor plans

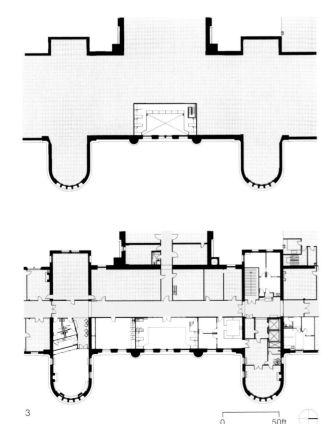

3

0   50ft

1

192

Mt. Tremper, New York
Zen Mountain Monastery
11,500 square feet
Design 2006/Scheduled completion 2009
Timber frame
Bluestone walls and wood siding, wood windows with operable louvers; interior finishes include floors of bluestone or bamboo, walls and ceilings are wood slats, and painted plaster board; energy sources for heating and cooling are geothermal and solar, with radiantly heated floors

Zen Mountain Monastery New Dragon Hall

Dragon Hall is a place for performances and exhibitions of Zen arts, a welcome center for those visiting on retreat, and a communal facility for resident monks. Sited along a path connecting residential cabins and the Monastery's Main House, it forms an entrance court and an edge for the meadow at the heart of the monastery grounds.

The building is composed of three elements: a long, narrow two-story component for visitor and communal facilities; a performance hall with a distinctive curved roof form; and a central circulation and exhibition space that originates in a stair at the east and extends to a sculpture garden at the west. Each element of the building program is sited in relation to adjacencies of use and harmony with the surrounding landscapes.

The ground level includes the entry, reception area, offices, and a monastery store. A curved wall, washed with daylight from skylights above, divides the performance hall and exhibition space. The performance hall has 150 seats with a portable stage for dance, Noh theater, and lectures, and can also be used as a space for meditation. The second floor accommodates a Hosan kitchen, monks' showers and laundry facilities, a multi-use space for yoga and children's activities, a gym, and a library and media center, which overlooks the meadow and entrance court.

Dragon Hall is constructed of a timber frame with exterior cladding of bluestone gathered on the site, and wood siding. Exterior walls are super-insulated, and window openings are protected by louvers that can be adjusted seasonally and daily in response to the movement of the sun. Solar panels capture the sun's energy, and flowing water provides geothermal heating and cooling. Every interior space is daylit and the arrangement of rooms around a central operable skylight provides continuous natural ventilation. Movable walls encourage the creation of environments adapted to specific uses. Many building elements, finishes, and systems are designed simply, to allow easy construction by monastery monks.

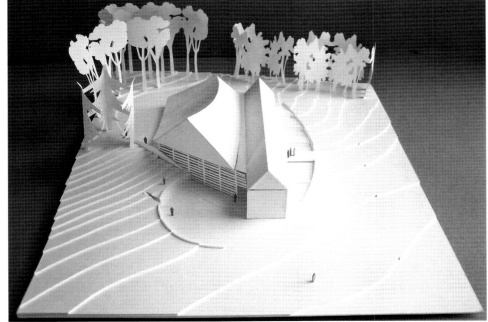

2

3

4

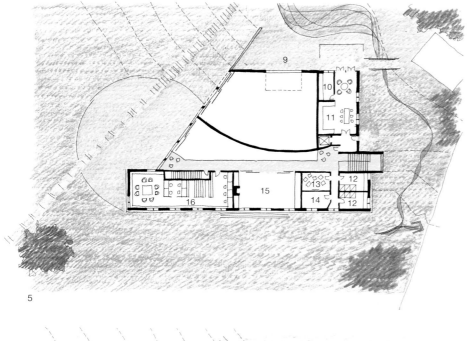

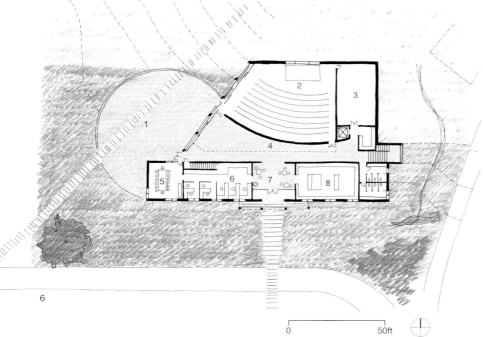

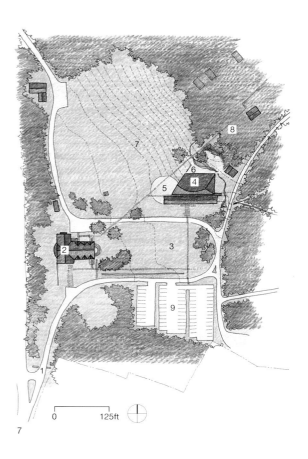

1 Sculpture garden
2 Hall of the Arts
3 Mechanical and storage
4 Exhibition gallery
5 Conference room
6 Office
7 Entrance lobby
8 Monastery store
9 Mountain viewing terrace
10 Laundry
11 Hosan kitchen
12 Shower
13 TV room
14 Gym
15 Multipurpose/practice room
16 Library and media rooms

5

6

0   50ft

1 Entrance gate
2 Main House
3 Entrance court
4 Dragon Hall
5 Sculpture garden
6 Mountain viewing terrace
7 Meadow
8 Path to monk's cabins
9 Parking

0   125ft

7

Zen Mountain Monastery, New Dragon Hall **195**

Baltimore, Maryland

Johns Hopkins University

146,000 square feet

Design 2006/Scheduled completion 2010

Existing concrete and steel structure, brick masonry bearing walls

New wood windows, glass and steel skylight, steel interior structure, new mechanical and electrical systems, glass partitions, carpet, terrazzo tile, and recycled marble floors

Johns Hopkins University Gilman Hall Renovation

This project is a reconfiguration of the historic Gilman Hall to accommodate the humanities departments, instructional spaces, and archeological collections. Built in 1915, Gilman is the first building of the Homewood Campus, and originally housed the university library and departmental offices.

The removal of library book stacks will allow for additional space to accommodate departmental needs. Reconfiguration and clarification of circulation systems, with new corridors, stairs, elevators, and accessible entrances, are designed to foster interaction.

The fifth-floor roof will be raised, and dormers removed. A tension-grid skylight will span the former central light well, covering a new atrium and creating a gathering space at the heart of the building. Glass catwalks connect circulation corridors on upper floors, and overscaled windows bring light into interior offices facing the atrium. The floor of the atrium will be paved in marble that is salvaged from the original book-stack structure.

New departmental offices on each floor will include faculty offices, seminar rooms, and graduate student workspace all grouped around the covered atrium. On the ground level of the atrium the archeological collection will be housed in glass vitrines, visible from the main circulation corridors and atrium above. This will be accessible to students in the adjoining workroom and seminar room. Historic rooms of significance, including Memorial Hall and the Hutzler Reading Room, will be restored to their original character, in contrast to new elements and spaces, which will be designed with simple modern finishes and lighting.

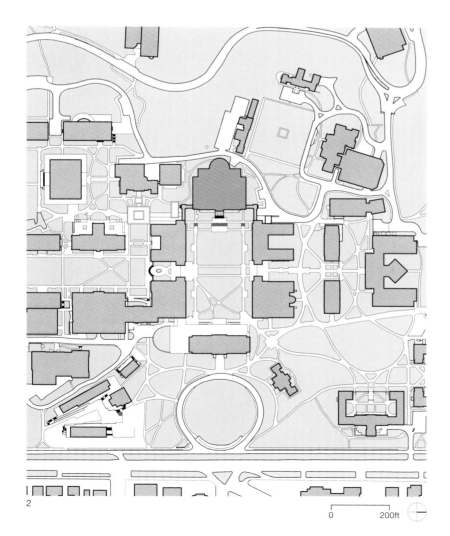

2

1 Archaeology collection and atrium
2 Site plan

0   200ft

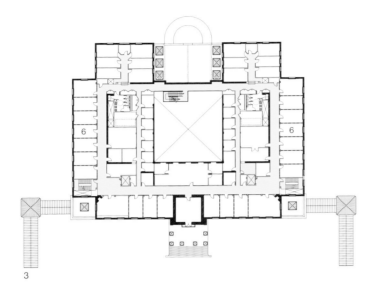

3

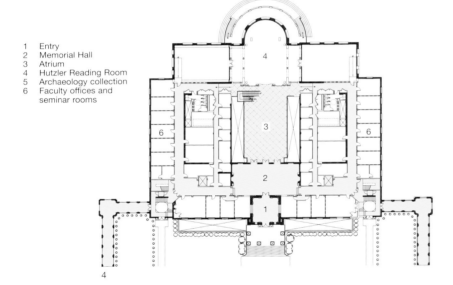

1 Entry
2 Memorial Hall
3 Atrium
4 Hutzler Reading Room
5 Archaeology collection
6 Faculty offices and
  seminar rooms

4

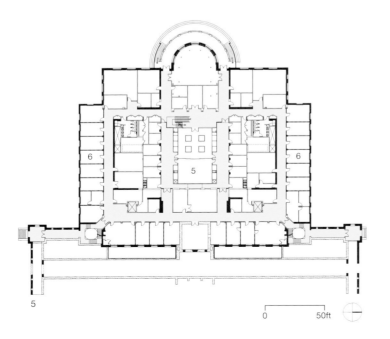

5

0   50ft

6

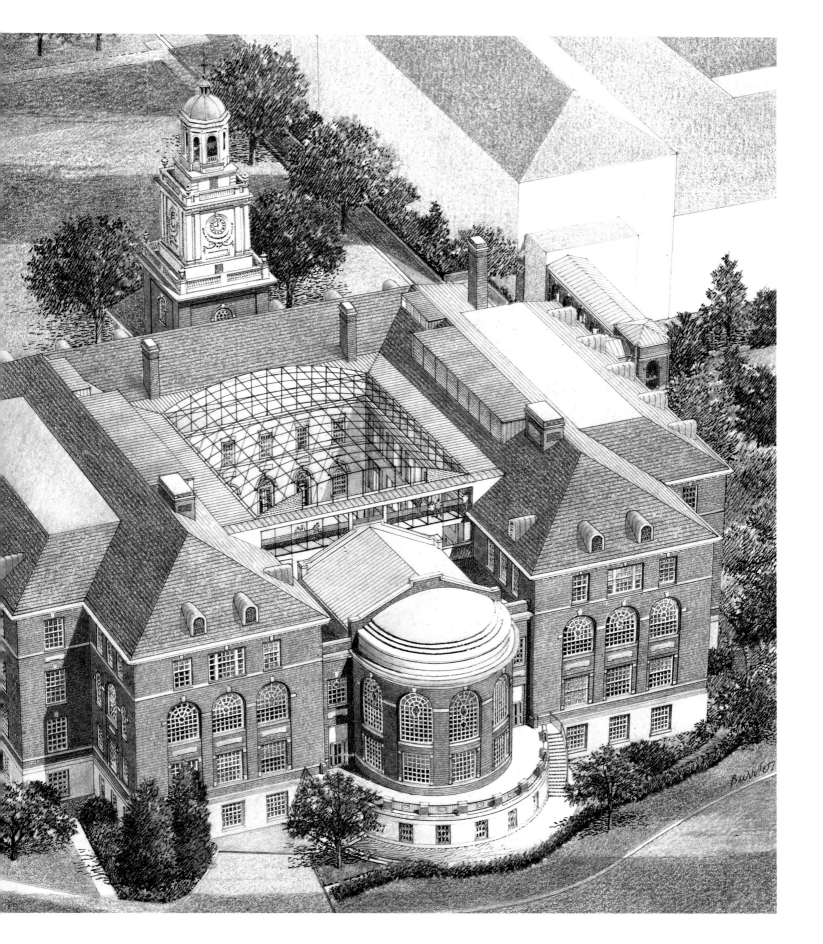

7 Longitudinal section
8 Transverse section through atrium
9 View from east
10 Atrium view

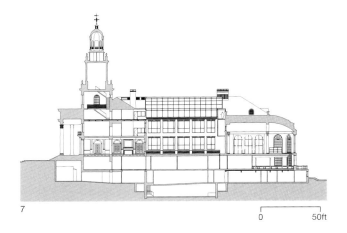

7

0   50ft

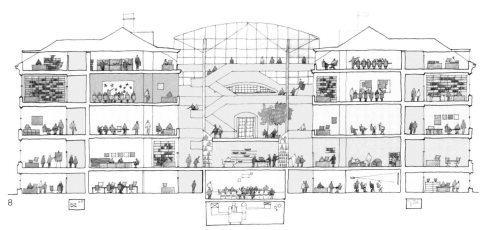

8

9

202

10

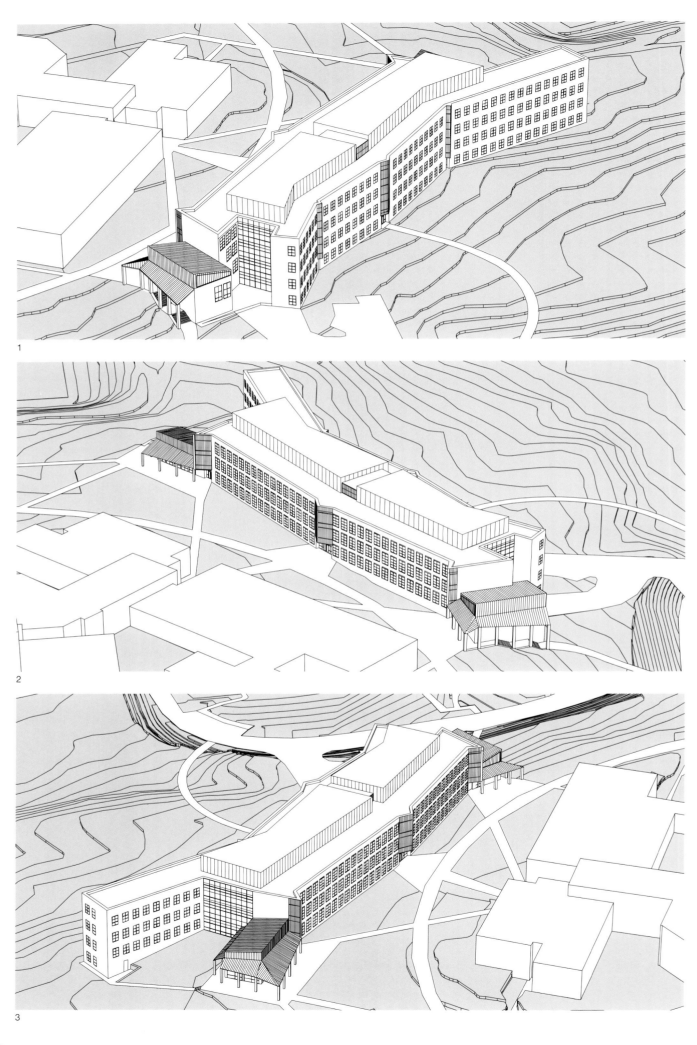

Old Westbury, New York

State University Construction Fund

134,000 square feet

Design 2006/Scheduled completion 2011

Steel structural frame, cast-in-place concrete floor slabs

Brick, precast concrete trim, standing seam metal roof, specialty glass, polished concrete floor, vinyl tile, carpet

State University of New York College at Old Westbury, New Academic Building

1 View from northwest
2 View from northeast
3 View from southeast
4 Site plan

The New Academic Building includes classrooms, faculty offices, computer labs, and administrative offices with shared instructional and support spaces for three schools: Arts and Sciences, Education, and Business.

The site is on the campus of the College of Old Westbury of the State University of New York, planned in the mid-1960s as a series of "academic villages," and then replanned in the mid-1970s as a centralized commuter college.

The New Academic Building defines a new entrance to the campus and is sited and designed to engage the buildings and landscapes of the campus. It is prominently located, visible, and accessible from the road and parking, the central open space and playing fields, the academic center and activities, and from the new residence halls.

The building is planned to permit flexible boundaries between the three schools, and to balance the fostering of faculty and student interaction with faculty privacy. The classrooms are oriented to the campus center, which accommodates shared and support functions. The offices are oriented to the woods and the residence halls while the student lounge and landscaped courtyard are oriented toward the campus open spaces. The lecture hall is located for direct access from the new campus entrance.

The exterior materials of the new building are selected for compatibility with the adjoining buildings: the east elevation is primarily a buff-colored brick; the west elevation is mainly red brick; the north and south elevations of the central band are a glazed curtain wall; and entrances are marked by the bay windows at the folds of the east and west elevations.

1 Bus-stop shelter
2 Upper entrance from campus
3 Lower entrance from campus
4 Campus center
5 Meadow court
6 Playing fields
7 Residence halls

4

0   200ft

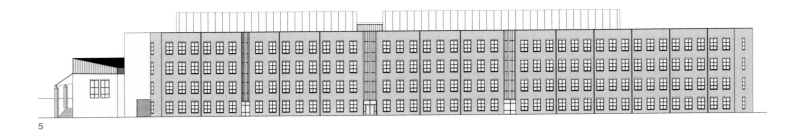

5

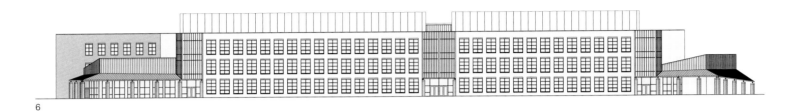

6

5 West elevation
6 East elevation
7 North elevation
8 South elevation
9 Section through student lounge and classrooms
10 Section through main stair
11 Section through lecture hall
12 Second-floor plan
13 First-floor plan
14 Ground-floor plan

7

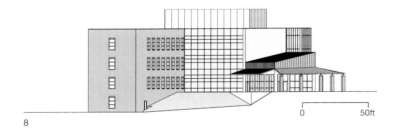

8

0   50ft

1 Main stair
2 Waiting areas
3 Common room
4 Lecture hall
5 Student lounge
6 Classrooms
7 Faculty office
8 Mechanical

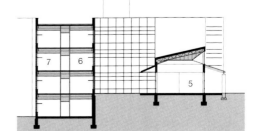

9

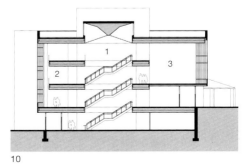

10

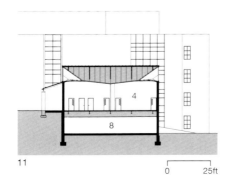

11

0   25ft

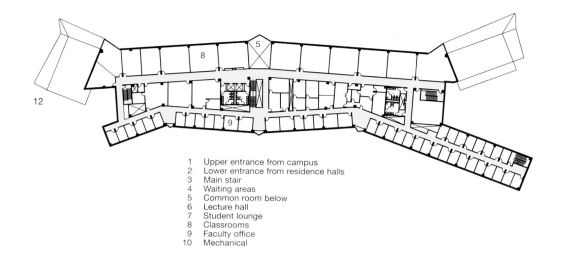

1 Upper entrance from campus
2 Lower entrance from residence halls
3 Main stair
4 Waiting areas
5 Common room below
6 Lecture hall
7 Student lounge
8 Classrooms
9 Faculty office
10 Mechanical

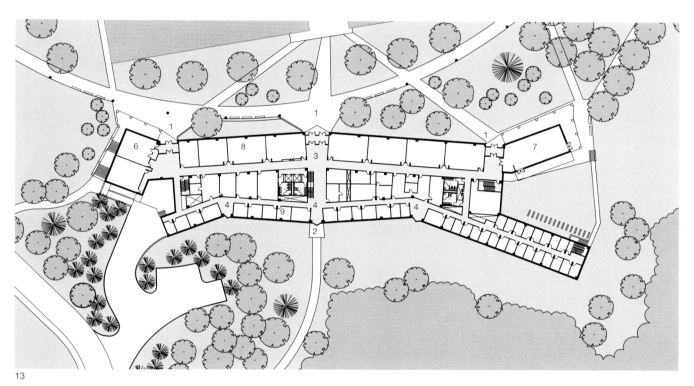

13

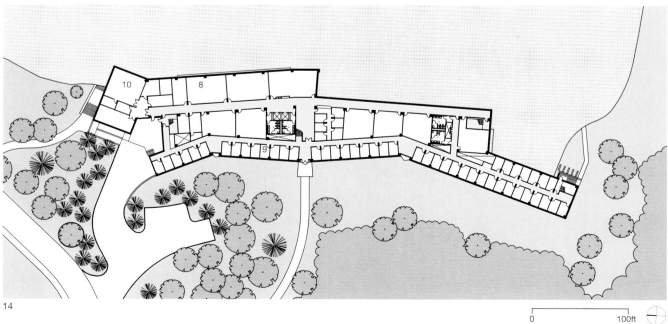

14

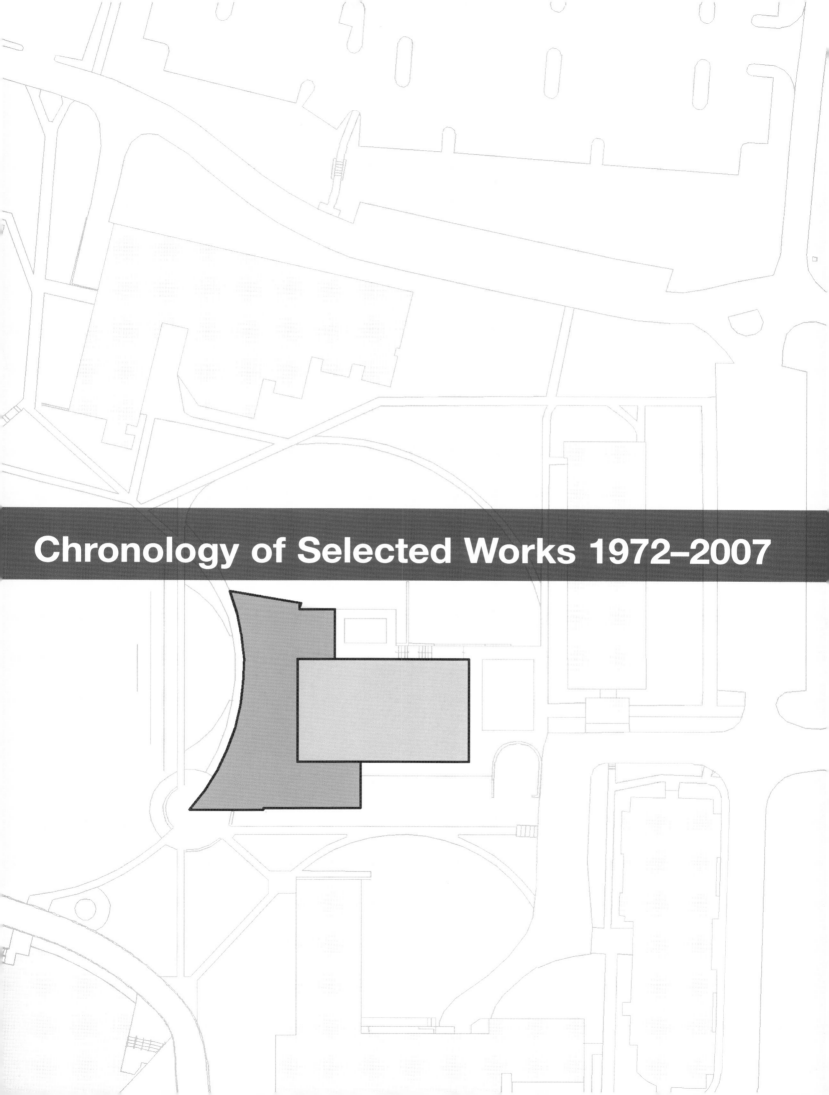

Chronology of Selected Works 1972–2007

Chronology

*Indicates projects featured in this book
(See Selected Works)

House on the Hudson River
Private client
Orange County, New York
Design: 1972
Completion: 1977

Woodstock Artists Association
Woodstock Artists Association
Woodstock, New York
Design: 1973

Apartment 1 in New York City
Private client
New York, New York
Design: 1974
Completion: 1975

Woodstock Master Plan and Sidewalk District Design
Town of Woodstock
Woodstock, New York
Design: 1974
Completion: 1979–1987

Chronology continued

Student Housing and Offices of the Controller
Columbia University
New York, New York
Design: 1974
Completion: 1978

Law Offices
Private client
New York, New York
Design: 1975
Completion: 1976

Apartment 2 in New York City
Private client
New York, New York
Design: 1975
Completion: 1975

Young Women's Christian Association
Young Women's Christian Association
Kingston, New York
Design: 1975
Completion: 1978

Cottage in Woodstock
Private client
Woodstock, New York
Design: 1976
Completion: 1977

William M. Mercer Employee Benefits Consulting Offices
William M. Mercer Incorporated
New York, New York
Design: 1976
Completion: 1977

Elementary School
The Town School
New York, New York
Design: 1977
Completion: 1978

Dental Offices
Private client
Woodstock, New York
Design: 1977
Completion: 1979

Banking Offices
Becker Warburg Paribas
New York, New York
Design: 1978
Completion: 1980

Margaretville Revitalization Project
Town of Margaretville
Margaretville, New York
Design: 1978
Completion: 1979

Apartment Renovation
Private client
New York, New York
Design: 1978
Completion: 1980

House in Garrison
Private client
Garrison, New York
Design: 1979
Completion: 1980

Science Library
Swarthmore College
Swarthmore, Pennsylvania
Design: 1980

Corporate Offices
Plechaty Companies
Cleveland, Ohio
Design: 1981
Completion: 1982

Columbia University, Computer Science Building
Columbia University
New York, New York
Design: 1981
Completion: 1983

House in Bedford
Private client
Bedford, New York
Design: 1981
Completion: 1984

Chronology continued

University of Virginia, Life Sciences Building
University of Virginia
Charlottesville, Virginia
Design: 1982
Completion: 1986

Controller's Office
Random House Inc.
New York, New York
Design: 1982
Completion: 1983

Executive Offices
Basix Incorporated
New York, New York
Design: 1983
Completion: 1984

Insurance Offices
Smith-Sternau Organization Incorporated
Washington, D.C.
Design: 1984
Completion: 1984

House on Long Island Sound

Private client
Westport, Connecticut
Design: 1984
Completion: 1985

House in Woodstock

Private client
Woodstock, New York
Design: 1984
Completion: 1985

House 1 on Martha's Vineyard

Private client
Martha's Vineyard, Massachusetts
Design: 1984
Completion: 1986

Riverside Buildings Renovation

The Penson Companies
Brooklyn, New York
Design: 1984
Completion: 1988

Studio House in Woodstock
Private client
Woodstock, New York
Design: 1985
Completion: 1986

House in Watermill
Private client
Watermill, New York
Design: 1985
Completion: 1987

McCarter & English Law Offices
McCarter & English, Attorneys at Law
Newark, New Jersey
Design: 1985
Completion: 1988–1997

House on Fishers Island
Private client
Fishers Island, New York
Design: 1985
Completion: 1988

New York Mercantile Exchange Building Renovation
Rockefeller Properties Incorporated
New York, New York
Design: 1985
Completion: 1988

Salisbury Town Hall
Town of Salisbury
Salisbury, Connecticut
Design: 1985
Completion: 1988

Princeton University, Computer Science Building
Princeton University
Princeton, New Jersey
Design: 1986
Completion: 1989

House in Remsenberg
Private client
Remsenberg, New York
Design: 1986
Completion: 1988

Dartmouth College, Mathematics and Computer Science Building

Dartmouth College
Hanover, New Hampshire
Design: 1986–1987

Levine, Huntley, Schmidt & Beaver Inc. Advertising Agency Offices

Levine, Huntley, Schmidt & Beaver Inc.
New York, New York
Design: 1986
Completion: 1988

Deming Street Café

Private client
Woodstock, New York
Design: 1986
Completion: 1989

Corporate Headquarters

Marsh & McLennan Companies Inc.
New York, New York
Design: 1988
Completion: 1990

Dartmouth College, Burke Chemistry Laboratory
Dartmouth College
Hanover, New Hampshire
Design: 1988
Completion: 1992

**Alvin Ailey American Dance Theater Foundation,
Dance Studios and Foundation Offices**
Alvin Ailey American Dance Theater Foundation Inc.
New York, New York
Design: 1989
Completion: 1989

House in Southampton
Private client
Southampton, New York
Design: 1989
Completion: 1992

Beach Club
Beach Point Club
Mamaroneck, New York
Design: 1990–1991

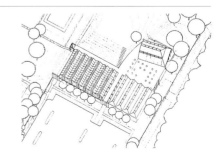

Long Island Rail Road Entrance Pavilion at Pennsylvania Station
Metropolitan Transportation Authority
New York, New York
Design: 1990
Completion: 1994

State University of New York at New Paltz,
Louis and Mildred Resnick Engineering Hall
State University Construction Fund
New Paltz, New York
Design: 1991
Completion: 1997

Case Western Reserve University, Adelbert Hall Administration Building
Case Western Reserve University
Cleveland, Ohio
Design: 1991
Completion: 1993

Dartmouth College, Computer Science Building Renovation and Addition
Dartmouth College
Hanover, New Hampshire
Design: 1991
Completion: 1994

Art Storage Facility
Bronx Council on the Arts and the Bronx Economic Development Corporation
Bronx, New York
Design: 1992
Completion: 1993

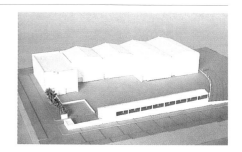

The College of Wooster, Ebert Art Center
The College of Wooster
Wooster, Ohio
Design: 1992
Completion: 1997

Dartmouth College, Roth Center for Jewish Life
Foundation for Jewish Life at Dartmouth College
Hanover, New Hampshire
Design: 1992
Completion: 1997

Independence Savings Bank, Headquarters Branch Bank
Independence Savings Bank
Brooklyn, New York
Design: 1993
Completion: 1995

Master Plan
White Flower Farm
Litchfield, Connecticut
Design: 1993
Completion: 1995

Independence Savings Bank, Court Street Branch Bank
Independence Savings Bank
Brooklyn, New York
Design: 1993
Completion: 1996

Brooklyn College Master Plan
City University of New York
Brooklyn, New York
Design: 1993
Completion: 1995

House 2 on Martha's Vineyard
Private client
West Tisbury, Massachusetts
Design: 1994
Completion: 1997

Primary School 54*
New York City Board of Education
Bronx, New York
Design: 1995
Completion: 1999

Columbia University, Lamont Doherty Earth Observatory Master Plan
Columbia University
Palisades, New York
Design: 1996

New York University, Deutsches Haus
New York University
New York, New York
Design: 1996
Completion: 1997

Olympic Village 2008 Master Plan
NYC 2008
New York, New York
Design: 1996–1997

U.S. Post Office and Courthouse*
U.S. General Services Administration
Brooklyn, New York
Design: 1996
Completion: 2003 (post office) and 2005 (courthouse)

Yale University, Sterling Divinity Quadrangle*
Yale University
New Haven, Connecticut
Feasibility study: 1996
Design: 1997
Completion: 2003

Smith College, Fine Arts Complex Planning Study
Smith College
Northampton, Massachusetts
Design: 1997

Columbia University, Undergraduate Life Sciences Laboratory*
Columbia University
New York, New York
Design: 1997
Completion: 2001

Muhlenberg Branch Library
New York Public Library
New York, New York
Design: 1997
Completion: 2001

Regional Television Studio and Broadcasting Facility
The Walt Disney Company
Orlando, Florida
Design: 1997

New York University, Languages and Literature Building*
New York University
New York, New York
Design: 1997
Completion: 2002 (phase 1 completed);
2005 (phase 2 completed); 2006 (phase 3 completed)

Institute for Advanced Study, Bloomberg Hall
Institute for Advanced Study
Princeton, New Jersey
Competition: 1998

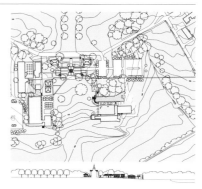

Chronology continued

Law Offices/Phase 3
McCarter and English
Newark, New Jersey
Design: 1998–1999
Completion: 1999

International Management Consulting Firm, Business Technology Office*
International Management Consulting Firm
Stamford, Connecticut
Design: 1998
Completion: 1999

Columbia University, Hamilton Hall*
Columbia University
New York, New York
Design: 1998
Completion: 2004

Columbia University, Lerner Hall
Columbia University
New York, New York
Design: 1999
Completion: 2000

Primary School 178*
New York City Board of Education
New York, New York
Design: 1999
Completion: 2001

**State University of New York at Albany,
College of Arts and Sciences Building***
State University Construction Fund
Albany, New York
Design: 1999
Completion: 2002

Dan M. Russell, Jr. United States Courthouse*
U.S. General Services Administration
Gulfport, Mississippi
Design: 1999
Completion: 2003

Smith College, Master Plan 2050
Northampton, Massachusetts
Design: 2000

Chronology continued

United States Courthouse
First Impressions/Entrance Renovation
U.S. General Services Administration
Des Moines, Iowa
Design: 2000

Franklin & Marshall College, Roschel Performing Arts Center*
Franklin & Marshall College
Lancaster, Pennsylvania
Competition: 2000
Completion: 2003

Arcadia University, Landman Library*
Arcadia University
Glenside, Pennsylvania
Competition: 2000
Completion: 2003

Yale University, Social Sciences and Engineering Planning Studies
Yale University
New Haven, Connecticut
Design: 2001–2003

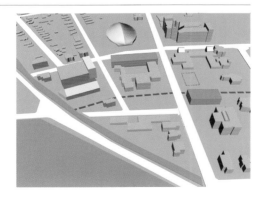

Franklin D. Roosevelt Presidential Library and Museum, Henry A. Wallace Visitor and Education Center*

National Archives and Records Administration
Hyde Park, New York
Design: 2001
Completion: 2004

Wyoming Seminary College, Performing Arts Center

Wyoming Seminary College Preparatory School
Kingston, Pennsylvania
Competition: 2002

Jewish Theological Seminary, Residence Hall

Jewish Theological Seminary
New York, New York
Design: 2002

University of Kentucky, Main Building*

University of Kentucky
Lexington, Kentucky
Design: 2002
Completion: 2004

Brown University, Strategic Framework for Physical Planning*
Brown University
Providence, Rhode Island
Design: 2002
Construction: 2006–

Arcadia University, Fine and Performing Arts Center
Arcadia University
Glenside, Pennsylvania
Feasibility study: 2003

The Riverside Buildings
Joralemon Realty/Pinnacle Group
Brooklyn, New York
Design: 2003–2006

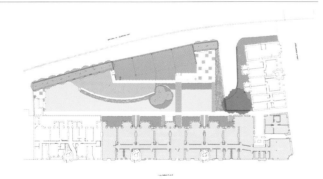

Temple Beth Elohim*
Temple Beth Elohim
Brewster, New York
Design: 2003
Completion: 2006

Federal Campus at St. Elizabeth's
U.S. General Services Administration
Washington, D.C.
Concept study: 2004

Church and Residential Tower
West Park Presbyterian Church
New York, New York
Design: 2004–2005

Dance New Amsterdam, School Studios and Theater*
Dance New Amsterdam
New York, New York
Design: 2004
Completion: 2006

Monroe High School Annex*
New York City School Construction Authority
Bronx, New York
Design: 2004
Scheduled completion: 2008

Chronology continued

Master Plan
Isabella Freedman Jewish Retreat Center
Falls Village, Connecticut
Design: 2005

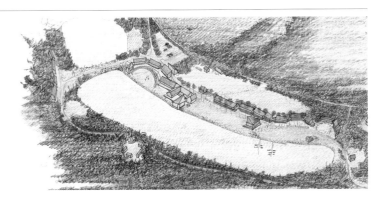

Development and Planning Prospectus/Boyers Facility
U.S. General Services Administration
Boyers, Pennsylvania
Design: 2005–2006

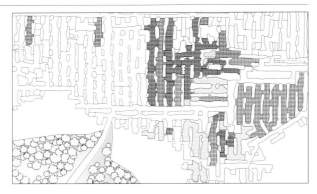

Avalon Morningside Park Apartments*
Avalon Bay Communities, Inc.
New York, New York
Design: 2005
Scheduled completion: 2008

American Museum of Natural History, Graduate and Postdoctoral Center*
American Museum of Natural History
New York, New York
Design: 2006
Scheduled completion: 2008

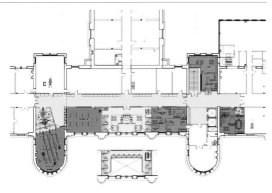

Vassar College, Old Observatory Renovation
Vassar College
Poughkeepsie, New York
Design: 2006
Scheduled completion: 2008

Zen Mountain Monastery, New Dragon Hall*
Zen Mountain Monastery
Mt. Tremper, New York
Design: 2006
Scheduled completion: 2009

Johns Hopkins University, Gilman Hall Renovation*
Johns Hopkins University
Baltimore, Maryland
Design: 2006
Scheduled completion: 2010

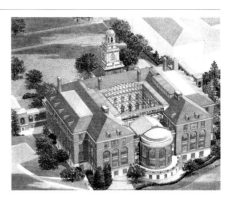

**State University of New York, College at Old Westbury,
New Academic Building***
State University Construction Fund
Old Westbury, New York
Design: 2006
Scheduled completion: 2011

Appendix

Firm Design Intentions

The R.M.Kliment & Frances Halsband Architects partnership was formed in 1972 in New York City. From the beginning, the firm has been characterized by the direct and continuing involvement of the partners in all aspects of the work, and by close collaboration between architects, consultants, and our clients. Today, there are four partners, two associates, and 20 architects, as well as supporting staff.

More than 50 design awards have been received, including the 1997 American Institute of Architects Firm Award, and the 1998 Medal of Honor from the New York Chapter AIA. Each of these is the highest honor given annually to one firm for creating consistently distinguished architecture. To mark that honor, in 1998, the monograph *R.M.Kliment & Frances Halsband Architects, Selected and Current Works* was published.

The guiding intentions of the practice were defined in the firm profile of that volume, and they remain the same today:

We intend our projects to be clearly conceived and carefully made places that engage the past and imply connections to the future. We believe it important that they engage the existing cultural and physical context, so that they become integral components of it; that they give direction to future uses and development, so that change and growth can be natural and coherent; that they fully develop the requirements and opportunities of program, so that they work well; and that their construction is congruent with available skills and funds, so that they are built well.

In the years since 1998, the firm's work has become more engaged in master planning and buildings for educational and civic purposes. It is increasingly involved in building for religious institutions, settings for even more rigorous investigation of values, and the translation of values into form. Guiding intentions are also influenced by a deeper concern for sustainability as a determinant of form, materials, and systems.

Our clients understand the power of place and the opportunity to use built form to express their values. For them, the discussion of balance between the preservation of history, and the desire for new creative approaches to community and culture form the basis of a design process, which results in forms that reflect those values.

Design is, in essence, the giving of form to values. *Reuben M. Rainey*

Professor of Landscape Architecture, University of Virginia

The building order develops naturally from the conditions of the site. *Romaldo Giurgola*

Introduction to competition entry for AIA Headquarters Building, 1964

… the past is altered by the present as much as the present is directed by the past. *T.S. Eliot*

Tradition and the Individual Talent

Understanding the "conditions of the site" requires a thorough investigation of what we see at the moment, and the forces that have made what we see. The history of a site reveals a set of responses to conditions over time. The geography, topography, ecology, and microclimate also inform the work and further the exercise of environmental responsibility. The cultural and political forces that continue to shape the surrounding environment provide a dynamic context for the future.

Finally, a community is an evolving work. The shared expectation of some degree of preservation, combined with the simultaneous urge to create new forms in a tightly controlled, closely examined, and highly contested environment, results in every new element being influenced by every existing condition, and every existing place being transformed by even the smallest degree of change.

Common themes of cultural evolution unite the projects included in this volume. An underlying consideration is the transformative effect of connections between new and existing buildings. Each project represents our continuing investigation of the transformative possibilities that new construction can bring to the perception and experience of existing places. The projects are studies of the world in microcosm, a continuing search for clarity of form that is coherent, consistent, and meaningful.

Biographies

Robert Kliment, FAIA
Partner

Robert Kliment, a founding partner of R.M.Kliment & Frances Halsband Architects, was born in Prague, Czech Republic. He earned his Bachelor of Arts from Yale in 1954, and then served in the U.S. Army in Europe. Kliment completed his Master of Architecture degree in 1959, also at Yale. Upon graduation, he received a Fulbright Fellowship to Italy, where he studied the history and evolution of buildings and urban spaces.

In 1961, Kliment moved to Philadelphia to work with Ehrman Mitchell and Romaldo Giurgola, then in the third year of their practice. In addition to his work there as designer and project architect, he began teaching with Giurgola in the Department of Architecture at the University of Pennsylvania. When Giurgola was appointed chairman of the Department of Architecture at Columbia University, Kliment moved to New York to open a Mitchell/Giurgola Architects' office, and joined Columbia University's faculty of architecture as a studio design critic.

In 1972, Kliment left Mitchell/Giurgola Architects to start the present practice with Frances Halsband in New York. He continued to teach as a visiting critic at Columbia University, University of Pennsylvania, and Yale University until 1984. He also taught joint studios with Frances Halsband at Harvard University, the University of Virginia, Rice University, and North Carolina State University.

Kliment has presented lectures on the firm's work to academic, professional, and lay audiences across the country. He has also served on numerous American Institute of Architects' committees and design awards juries, including service as chair of the year 2000 AIA National Honor Awards jury for architecture.

Frances Halsband, FAIA
Partner

Frances Halsband, a founding partner of R.M.Kliment & Frances Halsband Architects, was born in New York. She received her Bachelor of Arts from Swarthmore College in 1965, and went on to Columbia University, where she earned her Master of Architecture. After graduating in 1968, she traveled in Europe on a William Kinne Fellowship, to study medieval French cathedrals.

Halsband returned to New York and began her career with Mitchell/Giurgola Architects, leaving in 1972 to found the present practice with Robert Kliment. She began teaching in the undergraduate architecture program at Columbia University in 1975, and subsequently taught joint studios with Robert Kliment at Harvard University, the University of Virginia, Rice University, and North Carolina State University.

From 1991 to 1994, Halsband served as Dean of the School of Architecture at the Pratt Institute in New York. She has been visiting distinguished professor of design at many universities including Ball State, University of California at Berkeley, the University of Cincinnati, University of Illinois at Urbana-Champaign, University of Maryland, and University of Pennsylvania. She has been a visiting team member for the National Architectural Accrediting Board, as well as regional director of the Association of Collegiate Schools of Architecture. She has also served as architect advisor for Smith College from 1998 to 2003. Since 2002, she has been architect advisor to the board at Brown University.

Extensively engaged in professional and civic activities throughout the years, Halsband was the first woman to be elected president of the AIA New York Chapter. In addition to serving on many AIA-sponsored panels and design awards juries, she has served as president of the Architectural League of New York, commissioner of the New York City Landmarks Preservation Commission, chair of the AIA Committee on Design, chair of the AIA Honor Awards jury, and a member of the AIA Long Range Planning Advisory Group.

Halsband is currently a member of the Architecture Review Panel of the Federal Reserve Bank, and a board member of the Design History Foundation, Architectural League of New York, and President of the Woodstock Byrdcliffe Guild.

In addition to contributing several articles to *The Chronicle of Higher Education*, she has also been an advisory board member for *Crit*, Journal of the AIAS and *Praxis* journal, as well as an editorial board member for *Interiors* magazine, and the publisher of the Design History Foundation journal, *Places*.

Alejandro Diez, AIA
Partner

Alejandro Diez was born in Havana, Cuba. He received his Bachelor of Arts from Rutgers University in 1975, and his Master of Architecture from Columbia University in 1978. Upon graduation, he traveled in Europe and studied in Spain on a William Kinne Fellowship.

Diez began his career in New York in 1978 with R.M.Kliment & Frances Halsband Architects, becoming an associate in 1984 and a partner in 1997.

He is a member of the American Institute of Architects and is LEED accredited. Diez also sits on the AIA Committee on the Environment and the AIA Committee for Education. He was a guest lecturer at the Puerto Rico AIA Design Awards, and has served on Puerto Rico and Texas design awards juries.

Diez has led project teams for four Columbia University projects, including the Undergraduate Life Science Laboratory and Hamilton Hall. He was also team leader for the Arcadia University Library, Brown University Master Plan, the New York University Languages and Literature Building, Monroe High School, and Johns Hopkins University Gilman Hall.

Michael A. Nieminen, AIA
Partner

Michael A. Nieminen was born in Washington, D.C. He received his Bachelor of Environmental Design from The University of Florida in 1977 and his Master of Architecture from North Carolina State University, School of Design in 1983. He subsequently studied under the Henry Adams Scholarship.

Upon his graduation in 1983, he joined R.M.Kliment & Frances Halsband Architects, becoming an associate in 1986 and a partner in 1997.

Nieminen is a member of the AIA New York Chapter Committee on Architecture for Education, the AIA New York Chapter Committee on Architecture for Justice, the AIA New York Chapter Housing Committee, the Architectural League of New York, the National Trust for Historic Preservation of New York, the Preservation League of New York State, and the Society for College and University Planning.

He has lectured at the AIA Practice Management Conference, the AIA Committee on Architecture for Justice, and for the Society for College and University Planning. Nieminen also served on AIA Eastern New York, AIA Kentucky, and AIA Philadelphia design awards juries.

Nieminen's principal projects have included several planning studies and buildings for Yale, including the adaptive reuse of Sterling Divinity Quadrangle. He also has led the project teams for the two federal courthouses in Brooklyn, New York, and Gulfport, Mississippi, the university buildings for the New York State Construction Fund, Temple Beth Elohim, Avalon Morningside Park Apartments, and the American Museum of Natural History Graduate Center.

George K. George, AIA
Associate

George K. George was born in Kerala, India. He attended the Regional Engineering College in Trichy, India, where he earned his Bachelor of Architecture in 1988. George completed his Master of Architecture in 1991, at the University of Minnesota.

Upon graduation, George began his career at Bentz/Thompson/ Rietow in Minneapolis. In 1996, he relocated to New York to join R.M.Kliment & Frances Halsband Architects and became an associate in 2002.

From 2002 to 2005, he was a professor of architecture at the New York City College of Technology, where he currently remains an advisory board member. George is also a member of the AIA New York Chapter and has served on its Information Technology Committee since 1996.

George has worked on the team for the U.S. Post Office and Courthouse in Brooklyn, and has been project architect for Columbia University Hamilton Hall, Monroe High School, and the New Academic Building at Old Westbury College.

Carolyn J. Hinger, AIA
Associate

Carolyn J. Hinger was born in New Jersey. She received her Bachelor of Architecture from Mississippi State University in 2000. She has studied in England at the University of Plymouth and traveled throughout Europe.

Upon graduation, she joined RTKL Associates in Washington, D.C. After moving to New York in 2005, she joined R.M.Kliment & Frances Halsband Architects, becoming an associate in 2006.

Hinger is the recipient of the Brick Institute's Excellence in Design Award. She is also a member of the AIA New York Chapter and an LEED accredited professional. She has participated and led teams for volunteer organizations such as Canstruction and Rebuilding Together.

Hinger has been project architect for Avalon Morningside Park Apartments and Johns Hopkins University Gilman Hall.

Staff and Collaborators 1997–2007

Staff: Felix Ackerknecht AIA, Anna Agoston, Jack Allin, Jose Altamirano, Lori Baker, Andres Batista, Meital Ben-Shimon, Kristin Bergman, Rebecca Blackwell-Hafner, Emily Blumenthal, Michael Breault, Ralitza Boteva, John Breisky, Sarah Broughton, Catherine Brudz, Robert Bundy, William Caldera, Dalvine Charlton, Irene Cheng, Rawad Choubassi, Eric Chuderewicz, Eric Dempsey, Michael Deng, Alex Diez AIA, Anna Duncan, Richard Edwards, Richard L. McElhiney AIA, Matthew Fischesser, Jason Forney, Yetsuh Frank, Debra Fontenot, George K. George AIA, Joel Guerrero, Karla Gutierrez Glover, Jennifer M. Greene Associate AIA, Dewanto Gunawan, Lu-Min Guo, Frances Halsband FAIA, Yael Hameiri, Melora Heavey, Valerie Helman, Carol Hickey, Carolyn J. Hinger AIA, Jeffrey Hyman AIA, Ivy Jarrin, Steve Killian, Robert Kliment FAIA, David Kubik, Melissa Kuronen, Chi-Kwong Lau, Justin Lee, Wonsuk Lee, Elizabeth Leber, Karl A. Lehrke AIA, Michael Licwinko, Robert Litherland, Anne Marie Lubrano, Andrew Lynch, Maryse Maher, Michael Maher, Jonathan Mattox, Marlene Maxwell, Michael Maza, Tina Mesiti-Ceas, David S. Miller AIA, George Molato, Michelle Moseley, David H. Must AIA, Kirra Newman, Kurt Nieminen, Michael A. Nieminen AIA, Kevin O'Bryan, Ayanna Parker, Dorothy Pierson, Emily Pringle, Natalie Rebuck, Peninnah Ragasa, Rosemary Reilly, Basima Rum Associate AIA, Keif Samulski, Michael Shorr, William Singer AIA, Sasha Singh, Jordan Smith, Marissa Smith, Trish Solsaa, Gabriel Stock, Eve Szentesi, Tony Tai, Adam Taubman, Jenner Tobias, Ella Wang, Theodore Whitten, Beth Wieber, Nicholas Wilder, Wendy Wisbrun, Yara Wolos, Stanley Wong

Associated Architects

Canizaro Cawthon Davis (Dan M. Russell, Jr. United States Courthouse, Gulfport, M.S.)

James W. Potts Architects (University of Kentucky Main Building, Lexington, K.Y.)

Wank Adams Slavin Associates (U.S. Post Office and Courthouse, Brooklyn, N.Y.)

Dattner Architects (Primary School 178, New York, N.Y.)

Mechanical, Electrical, and Plumbing Engineers

Altieri Sebor Wieber Consulting Engineers, L.L.C.

Ambrosino, DePinto & Schmieder, Consulting Engineers, P.C.

Atkinson Koven Feinberg Engineers, L.L.P.

Bard Rao + Athanas Consulting Engineers, L.L.C

Eldridge & Associates, P.A.

Flack + Kurtz, Consulting Engineers, Inc.

I.M. Robbins, P.C.

Jack Green Associates

Perillo Associates Consulting Engineers

Watkins & O'Gwynn, P.A.

Staggs and Fisher, Consulting Engineers, Inc.

Structural Engineers

ADG Engineering

Cagley, Harman & Associates, Inc., Structural Engineers

Desimone Consulting Engineers

James Posey Associates Engineering & Surveying, Inc.

Richardson Structural Engineers

Robert Silman Associates, Structural Engineers

Severud Associates, Consulting Engineers, P.C.

Spencer-Engineers, Inc.

Lighting Designers

Brandston Partnership, Inc.

Hayden McKay Lighting Design, Inc.

Oxford Lighting Consultant

The Retec Group, Inc.

Tillotson Design Associates

Landscape Architects

Andropogon Associates, Ltd

Towers | Golde Landscape Architects

Donna Walcavage Landscape Architecture & Urban Design

L.A.D.A., P.C. Landscape Architecture/Planning

Todd Rader + Amy Crews Architecture, Landscape Architecture, L.L.C.

Signe Nielsen, Landscape Architects, P.C.

Weatherford/McDade, Ltd.

Awards 1997–2007

2007   **Educational Facilities Design Award of Excellence**

AIA Committee on Architecture for Education

Franklin D. Roosevelt Presidential Library and Museum, Henry A. Wallace Visitor and Education Center

Hyde Park, New York

2006   **Award of Merit**

AIA New York State

Franklin D. Roosevelt Presidential Library and Museum, Henry A. Wallace Visitor and Education Center

Hyde Park, New York

Honorable Mention for Unique Adaptive Re-use

Building Brooklyn Awards

U.S. Post Office and Courthouse

Brooklyn, New York

2005   **American Library Association Library Buildings Award**

AIA and ALA

Arcadia University, Landman Library

Glenside, Pennsylvania

Merit Award in Campus Heritage

Society for College and University Planning

Brooklyn College Master Plan

Brooklyn, New York

2004   **Merit Award**

Society for College and University Planning

Smith College Master Plan

Northampton, Massachusetts

Citation

AIA Committee on Architecture for Justice

Dan M. Russell, Jr. United States Courthouse

Gulfport, Mississippi

Honor Citation

AIA Mississippi

Dan M. Russell, Jr. United States Courthouse

Gulfport, Mississippi

Silver Award

American Society of Interior Designers, South Central Chapter

Dan M. Russell, Jr. United States Courthouse

Gulfport, Mississippi

Cultural Award of Merit

New York Construction

Franklin D. Roosevelt Presidential Library and Museum, Henry A. Wallace Visitor and Education Center

Hyde Park, New York

2003   **Religious Architecture Award**
        Faith & Form
        Yale University, Sterling Divinity Quadrangle
        New Haven, Connecticut

        Design Award
        AIA Connecticut
        Yale University, Sterling Divinity Quadrangle
        New Haven, Connecticut

2002   **Citation**
        AIA Committee on Architecture for Justice
        U.S. Post Office and Courthouse
        Brooklyn, New York

2000   **Award of Merit**
        American Institute of Architects New York State
        International Management Consulting Firm,
        Business Technology Office
        Stamford, Connecticut

        Religious Architecture Award
        Faith & Form
        Roth Center for Jewish Life at Dartmouth College
        Hanover, New Hampshire

1999   **American Architecture Award**
        Chicago Athenaeum
        Roth Center for Jewish Life at Dartmouth College
        Hanover, New Hampshire

1998   **1998 Medal of Honor**
        AIA New York Chapter
        R.M.Kliment & Frances Halsband Architects

        Design Award Citation
        U.S. General Services Administration
        U.S. Post Office and Courthouse
        Brooklyn, New York

        Certificate of Recognition
        AIA New York Chapter Committee on Architecture for
        Justice
        U.S. Post Office and Courthouse
        Brooklyn, New York

1997   **1997 Architecture Firm Award**
        American Institute of Architects
        R.M.Kliment & Frances Halsband Architects

Selected Exhibitions 1997–2006

2006   **"City of Culture: New Architecture for the Arts"**
(Dance New Amsterdam)
AIA New York Chapter
New York, New York

"Houses of Martha's Vineyard"
(House in the High Wood)
Boston Residential Design Trade Show, Boston Society of
Architects Gallery
Boston, Massachusetts

2005   **"New York Now"**
(Franklin D. Roosevelt Presidential Library and Museum,
Henry A. Wallace Visitor and Education Center)
AIA New York Chapter
New York, New York

2004   **"Columbia University's 250th Anniversary"**
(Columbia University Computer Science Building)
Columbia University
New York, New York

2003   **"Design New York"**
(U.S. Post Office and Courthouse)
AIA New York Chapter
New York, New York

2001   **"Giving Form to Values"**
(Arcadia University, Landman Library; Franklin & Marshall
College, Roschel Performing Arts Center; Franklin D.
Roosevelt Presidential Library and Museum, Henry A.
Wallace Visitor and Education Center; Yale University,
Sterling Divinity Quadrangle; Temple Beth Elohim)
I Space Gallery, University of Chicago, Urbana-Champaign
Chicago, Illinois

2000   **"New York State American Institute of Architects Design
Awards"**
(International Business Technology Management Office)
Brooklyn Museum of Art
Brooklyn, New York

"Religious Art and Architecture Design Awards"
(Roth Center for Jewish Life at Dartmouth College)
Interfaith Forum on Religion, Art and Architecture Conference
Andover, Massachusetts

"Exhibit"
(Roth Center for Jewish Life at Dartmouth College)
The American Institute of Architects National Convention
Philadelphia, Pennsylvania

"Exhibition of School Architecture"
(Primary School 54)
National School Boards Association 60th Annual Conference
Orlando, Florida

"Security in the Civic Realm"
(U.S. Post Office and Courthouse)
Foley Square Courthouse
New York, New York

1999   **"American Architecture Awards"**
(Roth Center for Jewish Life at Dartmouth College; College of
Wooster, Ebert Art Center; U.S. Post Office and Courthouse)
Chicago Athenaeum Museum of Architecture and Design
Chicago, Illinois

1998   **"Justice Facilities Review 1998–1999"**
(U.S. Courthouse and Post Office)
Traveling Exhibit
Third International Conference on Courthouse Design,
128th Congress of Correction

**"Precedent and Invention: New Courthouses in the Context
of Historic Courthouses"**
(U.S. Post Office and Courthouse)
U.S. Post Office and Courthouse
Brooklyn, New York

1997   **"Civics Lessons, Recent New York Public Architecture"**
(Entrance Pavilion, Long Island Rail Road at Pennsylvania
Station)
National Building Museum
Washington, D.C.

"Mastering McKim's Plan"
(Columbia University Computer Science Building)
Columbia University
New York, New York

"Street Furniture"
(Newsstand for the City of New York)
Municipal Art Society of New York
New York, New York

"Firm Award Exhibit"
(The Work of R.M.Kliment & Frances Halsband Architects)
AIA Architecture Firm Award Exhibit
AIA National Convention
New Orleans, Louisianna

"Federal Presence: Buildings for the Millennium"
(U.S. Post Office and Courthouse)
GSA Design Excellence Program
The Octagon
Washington, D.C.

Selected Publications 1997–2007

2007
Gunts, Edward, "Gilman Hall will grow a new heart of glass," *Baltimore Sun*, May 6, 2007 (Johns Hopkins University, Gilman Hall)

Strasberg, Hadiya, "Superior Court," *Traditional Building*, April, 2007 (U.S. Post Office and Courthouse)

Murdock, James, "Government Buildings: Open and Shut," *Architectural Record*, March, 2007 (U.S. Post Office and Courthouse)

2006
Feuer, Wendy and R.M.Kliment & Frances Halsband Architects, *United States Post Office and Courthouse, Brooklyn, New York*, U.S. General Services Administration, Washington, D.C., 2006 (U.S. Post Office and Courthouse)

Flanders, Steven (ed.), *Celebrating the Courthouse: A Guide for Architects, Their Clients and the Public*, W.W. Norton & Company, New York, 2006. (U.S. Post Office and Courthouse)

Hasanovic, Aisha, *2000 Architects*, The Images Publishing Group, Melbourne, 2006, p. 488. (Firm Profile and Selected Projects)

Stern, Robert A.M., David Fishman and Jacob Tiloye, *New York 2000: Architecture and Urbanism from the Bicentennial to the Millennium*, The Monacelli Press, New York, 2006. (Selected Projects)

Halsband, Frances, "Living and Learning: the Campus Redefined," *The Chronicle of Higher Education*, Vol. 52, No. 34, April 28, 2006, p. B10, B11, and B13.

Halsband, Frances, "A Master Plan for Retreat," *Faith & Form*, No. 1, 2006. (Isabella Freedman Jewish Retreat Center)

Murdock, James, "Civic Buildings: Acting Locally," *Architectural Record*, November 2006. (Franklin D. Roosevelt Presidential Library and Museum, Henry A. Wallace Visitor and Education Center)

"In the News: Dance New Amsterdam Leaps to Lower Manhattan," *eOculus*, April 4, 2006. (Dance New Amsterdam)

"In the News: Federal Courthouse and Post Office Restored in Brooklyn," *eOculus*, May 16, 2006. (U.S. Post Office and Courthouse)

2005
Moskow, Keith, *The Houses of Martha's Vineyard*, The Monacelli Press, New York, 2005. (House in the High Wood)

Halsband, Frances (ed.), "Campuses in Place," *Places: Considering the Place of Campus*, Vol. 17.1, Spring, 2005.

Halsband, Frances, "Charles Klauder's Brilliant Invisible Hand," *The Chronicle of Higher Education*, March 25, 2005.

Oppenheimer Dean, Andrea, "Rebuilding the Mississippi Gulf Coast: Architects Respond," *Architectural Record Online*, October 5, 2005.

"Brooklyn Courthouse Meticulously Restored," *New York Law Journal*, October 25, 2005. (U.S. Post Office and Courthouse)

"Original Design Revealed," *American School & University*, February, 2005. (Columbia University, Hamilton Hall)

2004

Nadel, Barbara A., *Building Security: Handbook for Architectural Planning and Design*, McGraw-Hill, New York, 2004. (Dan M. Russell, Jr. United States Courthouse)

"2003 Faith & Form Religious Architecture Award," *Faith & Form*, No. 1, 2004. (Yale University, Sterling Divinity Quadrangle)

"Best of 2004 Cultural Award of Merit—Franklin D. Roosevelt Presidential Library," *New York Construction*, December, 2004.

"Blocking Out the Future," *Brown Alumni Magazine*, May, 2004. (Brown University Strategic Framework for Physical Planning)

"Building Type Study: Arcadia University Landman Library," *Architectural Record Online*, December, 2004.

"Building Types Study: Dan M. Russell, Jr. United States Courthouse," *Architectural Record Online*, May, 2004.

"Building Type Study: Yale University Sterling Divinity Quadrangle," *Architectural Record Online*, 2004.

"Justice Is Not Blind," *Contract Magazine*, April, 2004. (Dan M. Russell, Jr. United States Courthouse)

"Open Court," *Building, Design & Construction*, May, 2004. (Dan M. Russell, Jr. United States Courthouse)

"Perspective: Frances Halsband," *Contract Magazine*, February, 2004.

"Renovation at Columbia's Hamilton Hall," *Preservation Online*, May 24, 2004.

"Status Symbol," *Contract Magazine*, February, 2004. (Arcadia University, Landman Library)

"Stunning Addition and Renovation to an Existing Library Celebrates Transition," *College Planning & Management Magazine*, April, 2004. (Arcadia University, Landman Library)

"The Revitalization of the Sterling Divinity Quadrangle," *Traditional Building*, March–April, 2004. (Yale University, Sterling Divinity Quadrangle)

Committee on Architecture for Justice, *2004–2005 Justice Facilities Review*, American Institute of Architects, Washington DC, 2004. (Dan M. Russell, Jr. United States Courthouse)

2003 "Adaptive Reuse: Connecting a Campus," *American School & University*, December, 2003. (Yale University, Sterling Divinity Quadrangle)

"Construction and Renovation Transform Two Spaces," *Yale Today*, Fall, 2003. (Yale University, Sterling Divinity Quadrangle)

"Roschel Performing Arts Center," *Architectural Record Online*, October, 2003. (Franklin & Marshall College, Roschel Performing Arts Center)

"Soundings: A Need Fulfilled," *Hudson Valley*, December, 2003. (Franklin D. Roosevelt Presidential Library and Museum, Henry A. Wallace Visitor and Education Center)

"The Second Coming of the Divinity School: Twelve Views on God and Man at Yale," *Yale Alumni Magazine*, September–October, 2003. (Yale University, Sterling Divinity Quadrangle)

"Theater Space: Lancaster Country," *Stage Directions*, November, 2003. (Franklin & Marshall College, Roschel Performing Arts Center)

2002 Hope, Eliza (ed.), *Museum and Art Spaces of the World: Volume 1*, The Images Publishing Group, Melbourne, 2001. (The College of Wooster Ebert Art Center)

"Roth Center for Jewish Life," *Wood Design & Building*, Winter, 2002. (Roth Center for Jewish Life at Dartmouth College)

"A Bronx School Negotiates the Slope of its Neighborhood," *Architectural Record Online*, February, 2001. (Primary School 54)

2000 Hope, Eliza (ed.), *Details in Architecture: Volume 2*, The Images Publishing Group, Melbourne, 2000. (Long Island Rail Road Entrance Pavilion at Pennsylvania Station)

Residential Spaces of the World: Volume 4, The Images Publishing Group, Melbourne, 2000. (House 2 on Martha's Vineyard)

"Brooklyn's History Meets its Future," *New York Construction News*, February, 2000. (U.S. Post Office and Courthouse)

"New Library Completes Central Campus," *designarchitecture.com*, October, 2000. (Arcadia University, Landman Library)

"New Views from 19th Century Court," *Correctional News*, November–December, 2000. (U.S. Post Office and Courthouse)

1999 Rhinehard, Raymond, *Princeton University: The Campus Guide*, Princeton Architectural Press, New York, 1999. (Princeton University, Computer Science Building)

"Island People," *House Beautiful*, June, 1999. (House 2 on Martha's Vineyard)

"Something Old, Something New—The Art of Preservation," *College Planning & Management*, August, 1999. (The College of Wooster Ebert Art Center)

1998 Dolkart, Andrew S., *Morningside Heights: A History of its Architecture and Development*, Columbia University Press, New York, 1998. (Columbia University, Computer Science Building; Columbia University, Frank S. Hogan Hall)

Rifkind, Carol, *A Field Guide to Contemporary American Architecture*, Plume, New York, 1998. (Columbia University, Computer Science Building)

Greer, Nora Richter, *The Architecture Transformed: New Life for Old Buildings*, Rockport Publishers, Beverly, 1998. (Case Western Reserve University, Adelbert Hall)

Sirefman, Susanna, and Keith Collie, *New York: A Guide to Recent Architecture*, Ellipsis Arts, Orange, 1998. (Entrance Pavilion, Long Island Rail Road at Pennsylvania Station; Columbia University, Computer Science Building)

Educational Spaces: Volume 1, The Images Publishing Group, Melbourne, 1998. (College of Wooster Ebert Art Center; Columbia University, Computer Science Building; Princeton University, Computer Science Building)

Master Architects Series III: R.M.Kliment & Frances Halsband Architect— Selected and Current Works, The Images Publishing Group, Melbourne, 1998.

Justice Facilities Review, 1998–1999. (U.S. Courthouse and Post Office)

"Equal Partners—Men and Women Principals in Contemporary Architectural Practice," *Smith College, Exhibition Catalogue*, 1998. (The College of Wooster, Ebert Art Center; International Management Consulting Firm, Business Technology Office Prototype)

1997 Halsband, Frances, "On Partners," *Practices* 5/6, 1997.

"1997 Best and Brightest American Architects," *Building Stone*, 1997.

"Architecture Firm Award Winner, R.M.Kliment & Frances Halsband Architects," *AIArchitect*, February, 1997.

"Architecture Firm Award Winner, R.M.Kliment & Frances Halsband Architects," *Architectural Record*, May, 1997.

"Entrance Pavilion, Long Island Rail Road at Pennsylvania Station," *Lotus 92*, July, 1997.

"Independence Savings Bank Headquarters Branch," *Interior Design*, May, 1997.

"Mastering McKim's Plan," *Columbia University, Exhibition Catalogue*, 1997. (Columbia University, Computer Science Building)

"The College of Wooster Art Museum," *Dialogue*, September–October, 1997.

Photography and Drawing Credits

Unless otherwise indicated, all site and floor plans by R.M.Kliment & Frances Halsband Architects.

Introduction

Page 7, 8: Cervin Robinson

Page 9: all photos by Cervin Robinson, except top image by Lori Stahl

Page 10, from top: Lori Stahl, Peter Mauss/ESTO, Peter Aaron/ESTO, Cervin Robinson

Primary School 54

All photos by Peter Aaron/ESTO

U.S. Post Office and Courthouse

All photos by Cervin Robinson

Yale University, Sterling Divinity Quadrangle

All photos by Cervin Robinson

Columbia University, Undergraduate Life Sciences Laboratory

All photos by Peter Aaron/ESTO

New York University, Languages and Literature Building

All photos by Ruggero Vanni

International Management Consulting Firm, Business Technology Office

All photos by Peter Aaron/ESTO

Columbia University, Hamilton Hall

All photos by Ruggero Vanni, except pages 76 (3) and 80 (10) by R.M.Kliment & Frances Halsband Architects

Primary School 178

All photos by Peter Mauss/ESTO

SUNY Albany College of Arts and Sciences Building

All photos by Ruggero Vanni

Dan M. Russell, Jr. United States Courthouse

All photos by Cervin Robinson

Franklin & Marshall College, Roschel Performing Arts Center

All photos by Lori Stahl, except page 107 (6) by Walter Smalling

Arcadia University, Landman Library

All photos by Cervin Robinson except page 110 (1) by Lori Stahl

Franklin D. Roosevelt Presidential Library and Museum, Henry A. Wallace Visitor and Education Center

All photos by Cervin Robinson

University of Kentucky, Main Building

All photos by Cervin Robinson, except page 141 (7) by R.M.Kliment & Frances Halsband Architects

Brown University, Strategic Framework for Physical Planning

Renderings by Frances Halsband

Dance New Amsterdam, School Studios and Theater

All photos by Ruggero Vanni

Temple Beth Elohim

All photos by Ruggero Vanni

Monroe High School Annex

Renderings by Brian Burr

Avalon Morningside Park Apartments

Renderings by Brian Burr

American Museum of Natural History, Graduate and Postdoctoral Center

Page 190 (2) by R.M.Kliment & Frances Halsband Architects

Zen Mountain Monastery, New Dragon Hall

Renderings by Brian Burr

Johns Hopkins University, Gilman Hall Renovation

All renderings by Brian Burr

Page 202 (8) sketch by Frances Halsband

Index

Every effort has been made to trace the original source of copyright material contained in this book. The publishers would be pleased to hear from copyright holders to rectify any errors or omissions.

The information and illustrations in this publication have been prepared and supplied by R.M.Kliment & Frances Halsband Architects. While all reasonable efforts have been made to source the required information and ensure accuracy, the publishers do not, under any circumstances, accept any responsibility for errors, omissions and representations expressed or implied.